Danny Cole is the founder of The Formula Coaching Systems, Director of Sales for New Beginning Financial Group, a Certified NLP Master Practitioner, a Certified Hypnotherapist, a Certified Life Coach, an Author, and Motivational Speaker.

He has been in the sales industry for over 18 years and is dedicated to helping others achieve their financial goals as well as any other goals in life they may have. His passion is to motivate, inspire, and empower others to overcome the self-imposed limitations that are holding them back and truly reach their fullest potential.

The Formula For Success In Sales

Your Complete Guide To Selling

Your Product To ANYONE, ANYWHERE, ANYTIME!

Publication date 2016

Written by: Danny Cole

Published by: Cole-Han Publishing

theformulacoach.com

theformulacoachingsystems.com

ISBN 978-0-692-79812-6

Library of Congress Control Number: 2016917554

Special thanks to all of the managers that have hired me over the years and allowed me to learn and grow and develop my skills.

Thank you to all of the Top Sales Professionals and Top NLP Experts around the world that allowed for this book to be written, because of their unmatched knowledge, this book will enable their proven techniques to be easily learned and reproduce the same unbelievable results. Last and most importantly to Solah Han who has been there and encouraged me and supported me throughout this entire process, and as always thank you God for all things are possible with you.

Table of Contents

<u>Chapters</u>   <u>Page</u>

Preface

Do you want to make a lot of money in sales? Imagine if you could learn how to earn more in the next 6 months more than you have in the last 6 years. How would that improve your personal life? How would that improve your business life? What are some things you would do differently? What I have learned in almost 20 years of sales experience from selling cars, real estate, MLM, personal development products, and everything in between is that a successful, simple, easy to follow formula is the best way to achieve a desired result. Do not complicate the process. Complication equals overwhelm and overwhelm equals BROKE! And you do not want to be broke do you? You see, there is opportunity everywhere you turn and once you discover the formula for success in sales, you can take advantage of it all. Your income potential will become unlimited!

Have you ever noticed how most books on teaching the process of sales, or anything that is teaching you a process on how to do something for that matter, leaves you more confused by the time you finish than when you first started? It's almost as if the author feels the compelling need to sound extremely intelligent by creating an intricate but complicated long drawn out process, all the while using words that you need to continually use Google to search the definition of. It is almost as if they do it to create some sort of an illusion of credibility on the subject. I honestly think after they finish writing their complicated book, they sit back and quietly laugh and say to themselves, "Now I will write part two of this book to explain part one and make a fortune!"

You see, this book is written differently. This book was written with only one goal in mind, for you to easily become extremely successful and make lots of money. To accomplish this goal, I wrote this book in laymen's terms, so it does not matter if you are just entering into the lucrative field of sales or are a seasoned professional, you can easily apply the formula for success in sales and achieve the financial freedom you are searching for.

The more you read this book, the more your confidence will grow and because of the straightforward, powerful information and techniques written inside, you will feel so confident in your ability to close every sale so easily that you will grow more and more excited with every person you speak to. You might even find yourself using them on people you are not even trying to sell. Also, the more information and techniques you learn in this book, the more money you will earn, and that sounds good doesn't it?

This book contains the most influential and hypnotic NLP language patterns ever created, which are being used by the CIA, the Secret Service, and other such secret agencies. The most powerful secrets from the most successful sales professionals around the world are written inside this book. You will learn the incredibly powerful NLP sales processes from greeting to closing, to absolutely dominating the sales industry and having customers literally handing you their business.

NLP (Neuro-Linguistic Programming) is the study of human excellence and persuasion. It is absolutely powerful and used by almost every top sales professional (and speakers) including Grant Cardone, Brian Tracy, Tom Hopkins, Anthony Robbins, Les Brown, the late Zig Ziglar, the government, recruiters, and countless others. If they are all using it to get the results they want, shouldn't you? NLP combines approaches from psychology, brain research, and complex systems theory to provide a new way of assisting customers to make satisfying purchases.

If you really think about it, no one enters into the sales profession; a profession majorly dominated by a commissions-only pay, and say to themselves, "I do not plan on being successful. I am ok with only earning $30,000 or $40,000 a year." Unfortunately, this is what the majority of sales "professionals" earn.

The reason someone enters into the honorable profession of sales is for two reasons: one, they have a passion for people, and two, they want to earn what they are worth, not what someone else says they are worth. But if this is truly the case, then why are so many sales professionals not successful? The answer is simple. They do not know the formula for success in sales. What happened was they learned a poor way of implementing the sales process and continued to do it over and over again, just expecting to become successful over time. Do you know the definition of insanity? "Doing the same thing over and over and expecting different results." That is what most salesmen do.

You see, it's like this, the first time I learned how to drive a manual transmission, I stalled and jerked and ground the gears so much I thought something was wrong with the car, not my attempt at driving it. But fortunately, I was smart enough to realize that the problem wasn't with the car because other people drove the same car and achieved great results. I asked someone who received great results how to correct the problem I was having and learned how to successfully operate the vehicle. I noticed a problem in my application of technique, asked someone who had a successful technique, and then applied what I learned. That simple.

Instead of most salesmen admitting they may not know the best formula for success in sales and asking for help, they often think to themselves, and are not shy about telling you either, that it is the market's fault or some other unseen factor that is the reason for them not earning more money and providing for their families the way they want. The majority of low income salesmen are like this. They would rather give excuses for why they are not closing deals instead of asking for help to improve their skills. All of the top earning sales professionals are constantly learning and honing their skills. That is why they are at the top. If you do not believe me, go and ask them.

The sales industry is the number one industry in the world for those who want to create unlimited wealth for themselves. Once you know the formula for success in sales, it is easy. It is the only field I know of where you can make an excess of $100,000 a year without a degree, or even a high school diploma for that matter.

I remember being in a Saturday morning sales meeting at Bill Heard Chevrolet back in 1999, and the GM asked everyone, "Who wants a raise?" Everyone, obviously thinking he was about to increase the percentage we were paid per vehicle, raised our hands. He then said, "Then get off your ass and go sell something!" The sales industry is also the only industry that I know of where, if you want a raise, you can practically get it instantly. All you have to do is get off your ass and sell more!

If you are already in the field of sales or are considering going into the field, let me begin by telling you that you are among a special group that makes the world go round. If it wasn't for you, nothing would get bought or sold. If it wasn't for you, a product would just sit there on the shelf collecting dust, cars would just be hunks of metal rusting on the lot, and jets would only rest in their bays with anywhere to go.

If you are in sales, you should walk with your head held high and chest boldly displayed knowing the world as we know it would not exist if it wasn't for you. Because of you, the world is a better place. A place of opportunity and growth, a place where people survive and thrive, a place where others people's problems are solved and their lives made easier and more enjoyable. All because of you.

As I mentioned earlier, sales is a field you can easily make extremely large amounts of money and completely change your life. You see, once your successful formula for driving was discovered, it was able to be reproduced over and over again with precision and ease. Success in sales is the same way. Once you discover the formula for success in sales in the pages of this book and apply them, you can reproduce the results over and over again

If you, like me, get excited about sales and the opportunity to help others and make a great living doing it, then go ahead and smile and get ready to quickly and easily have your life change, forever because no matter where you go or what you sell, you can apply these powerful techniques and achieve the same results.

Your income potential is only limited by what you know and what you apply. So get ready to learn and start applying today, the formula to make all of your financial dreams come true. Once you have tapped into the formula for success in sales, your possibilities are endless.

CHAPTER 1

ATTITUDE IS EVERYTHING!

"Your attitude will make or break a sell."

Guaranteed Paycheck

Sales is one of the most fun, exhilarating, and lucrative professions in the world and for some it can be one of the scariest. It can be especially scary if you are new to the field. Why can it be one of the scariest fields if you are new? I'm glad you asked. While some wouldn't have it any other way others feel an extreme amount of stress from not having a "guaranteed" paycheck. They are scared to death due to the fact most sales jobs are commission only and based upon their skills. What it simply boils down to is they do not believe in themselves and their abilities. They would rather someone tell them what they are worth based upon their position at a "normal" job. The sales superstars of the world do not want to be paid by the hour. They do not want someone telling them they are only worth a predetermined amount of money per hour. They would rather prove their worth. And that is why you should love it! You get to prove your worth!

But first. What is a guaranteed paycheck? Someone telling you that if you work (x) hours you will be paid (x) dollars? Someone telling you before your retirement date that you are fired and will not receive your retirement benefits or pension? Which is now common place in the work industry. Don't believe me, just ask around and you will hear sad story after sad story of it happening. Someone telling you if you work forty hours a week for forty years that you will make them rich while you receive little to nothing in return. Unless of course you are investing wisely. And let's face it, most people working "normal" jobs are not investing wisely or even investing at all for that matter. Why? Because they are simply not making enough money to invest. With all the dept., bills, gas and grocery prices, and let's not forget taxes, continuing to go up, up, and up who has enough left over to invest? The ones who are successful in sales, that's who!

Everyone else is stuck in the hope of the 40 X 40 promise. If you work forty hours a week for forth years you will retire with forty percent of your income. But, not the successful sales people. They will not settle for 40 X 40 promise. They want more. They expect more. They demand more and guess what? They will get more.

They are the ones who take several vacations a year. They are the ones who drive the highline cars. They are the ones able to invest large sums of money with high returns. They are the ones everyone comes to for advice. Successful salespeople are the ones bouncing around the office or dealership stress free and happy as can be. Why? Is it because they know something everyone else doesn't? You're damn right that's why. Successful salespeople know that the right attitude is worth its weight in gold. In fact, according to a Stanford Research Institute study by Psychologist Carol Dweck, success is comprised of 88% attitude and only 12% education. IQ is a less important factor compared to attitude when it comes to success. I also read somewhere that sales superstars will prosper in any industry where others seem to be struggling due to one factor. Their attitude! Your attitude will determine your altitude.

15

You're Attitude

There are many things in life that are out of your control; the weather, the stock market, if your spouse has had a good day or is in a good mood, or how people react to your product or service. But, what you are in 100% complete and total control of is your attitude. Attitude is everything. You see, your attitude is the key that unlocks the door and allows you to achieve your greatest potential in life. Your attitude will determine how you perceive the world and all the opportunities it has to offer. It's not what we go through but how we perceive it that makes the difference.

What is attitude? I Googled the definition of attitude and this is what it said, "A settled way of thinking or feeling about someone or something, typically one that is reflected in a person's behavior." Your attitude about yourself is portrayed by how you perceive life and how others perceive you. Think about it for a moment. If you have a bad attitude and believe, because an attitude is a belief in someone or something, that the economy is in the toilet and no one is buying anything, then how do you think your sells would look by the end of the month? They would be a direct reflection of your attitude

Everything in life is a direct reflection of your attitude towards it. Reality is relative to the perception you perceive. Your relationships. Your health. Your finances. Everything. If you are in a relationship and believe that everyone cheats and lies then your attitude will be a direct reflection of it. You will not trust the other person. You will question every move they make. Every gesture and sentence will be broken down and analyzed. You will more than likely cheat and lie, also. Why? Because if you think your significant other has stepped outside of the sacred boundaries of the relationship then you can too. And now let me ask you this. How do you think that relationship is going to be? Do you think it will last? Do you think it will be one of peace and happiness? Is it a relationship you yourself would be excited to be in? No. Of course not. Change your attitude and you will change your life. Because your attitude will determine what you believe and what you believe will determine what you see in the world.

It's like this. Have you ever purchased a car and then noticed the same make and model everywhere you went? You never noticed it before, but after you bought it you couldn't even go on a short trip to the corner store without seeing another one. And, sometimes you would even see it in the same exact color, wouldn't you? This is the same way with your attitude. Whatever you believe to be true your mind will look for supporting details to back up your belief. No matter how sane or insane the belief is your mind will work to find supporting evidence to prove to yourself that you are right. Some people have the attitude that it is difficult to become a millionaire. Some believe that businesses are not doing well and that you cannot make any money in the current market. Be careful what you believe.

The world wealth report by Cagemini and RBC Wealth Management stated that 920,000 new millionaires were created in 2014. Think about that for a moment. 920,000 new millionaires were created in 2014 alone. If you are not a millionaire yet don't worry because new millionaires are being created at an average of just over 2,520 every single day. That combined with the previous number of high net worth individuals, individuals having at least $1 million of investable assets, puts the worldwide total at 14.6 million millionaires. Take some time and let that sink in. 14.6 million millionaires worldwide. If 14.6 million people can do it so can you. That is if you have the right attitude and know the right formula. Remember you are not trying to reinvent the wheel. All you have to do is follow a proven formula for success. Which is simple. Understand how someone else became successful and duplicate it.

Belief And Attitude

One thing you have to remember is your attitude is a belief. It is a belief about someone or something based upon past experiences or opinions and is reflected in your actions. So, in reality a belief is only a thought that has been reinforced. A belief isn't necessarily true or false it is just what you believe to be true or false. Take for example. You may believe that chocolate ice-cream is the best flavor of ice-cream ever created since the creation of ice-cream. Why? Well, there could be several reasons for this belief. It could have been the flavor you ate as a child on a warm summer day with your family at the zoo. It could be because you are allergic to all the other flavors. Who knows?

But, someone else could believe that strawberry flavor ice-cream is the best flavor under the sun. And it could be because it was his/her best friend's favorite flavor. Everyone believes different things for different reasons. It doesn't mean they are right and you are wrong or that you are right and they are wrong, all it means is you have a difference of opinions. That's it.

So, now that you know a belief is only a thought that has been reinforced that means you now also know how to begin to create a new belief or attitude. That's right. You reinforce the belief or attitude you want or need to have to become successful. Really think about this question for a moment. What type of attitude would be the most advantageous for you to become successful in what you sell? Would having an attitude that your product is the best product under the sun and that there is no other product in this world that can even come close to providing your customers or client's needs better, be advantageous for you? How about the attitude that you completely and totally believe in yourself? Or, that you completely believe in your company and what they stand for?

When I first got started in the business of sales, well let me take that back. When I first got into the business of "sales" I was in middle school. How I got started was I would go to the only little country store waaaaayyy out in the country where I grew up, now known as Chattahoochee Hills and purchase these little 10 cent pieces of candy called "Airheads." It was a type of sweet mouthwatering taffy that was thin and about 5 inches long and 1 inch wide wrapped in an attractive wrapper that screamed "open me now and eat me" that everyone

loved, and I would sell them on the school bus and at
school for 25 cents each. (Not a bad markup.) I even
remember "selling" this one kid on sharing with me the
piece of candy he just purchased from me, because I
didn't want to eat into my profits. (Pun intended) I
learned at the tender age of eleven that there was money
to be made in sales. I mean here I was selling candy at
more than double the markup than the markup at the
convenient store. That is when I also learned that
people buy with emotions and justify with logic. We will
talk more about that later.

Now, back to the original story. You must believe in
your product. When I first got into car sales I worked at
Bill Heard Chevrolet. This place was a real turn and
burn kind of place. In my six months of being there I
had to have seen at least 30 or more salespeople come
and go. The GM was one of those hardnosed, very
rude, and arrogant kind of managers. He hurled insults at
everyone in the Saturday morning sales meeting like it
was a game, had you working bell to bell every day, and
every holiday, especially if you were new. This was my
first official sales job, other than selling Amway, and I
loved everything about it, other than of course the GM.
I worked sixty hours a week, got to dress nice every
single day, everyone called me sir, made a ton of money,

and the rush I got from each sale was unmatched to anything else in existence. I have to warn you, sales is a drug. You feel on top of the world when you are selling. You feel invincible. You feel as if you can conquer anything. You are going to love it.

I gained a substantial amount of knowledge about sales and the different personality types in the six months I worked there. It was a great place to start and I truly believed in the product. I was selling between 10-15 cars a month and making good money doing it, especially for a kid who was barley 21 at the time. But the management was some of the worst I had ever encountered to this day. So, I decided to take what I learned and continue on my new found path in sales to a different dealership. After all, car dealerships were and still are everywhere. I left the GM product behind and went to sell cars at the Hyundai dealership ten minutes away. Now keep in mind this was in the late 90's and the Hyundai product was not where it is today. Today it is some of the best made vehicles out there but back then, it wasn't. They were known as the "throwaway" cars. You can buy them for cheap and they would last you a little while and then you could just throw it away because you only paid something like ten grand for a brand new car.

I went there because I was intrigued about the cars being so inexpensive and thought, "Man I could really sell a lot of these things easy!" Plus another salesman, who used to work at Bill Heard alongside me told me that he was making seven thousand a month there selling these "throwaway" cars. But, when I got there I heard about all these cars going into the shop for all sorts of repairs and customers complaining, and I thought to myself, "Is this really something I would feel good about selling?" I just did not like the feeling it gave me in the pit of my stomach. And this is where I quickly learned, if you do not believe in what you sell, then you will go broke.

My sells where almost non-existent. I just did not feel right about selling someone a product that I did not trust or believe in myself and believe me my sales were a reflection of it. I went from selling 15 – 20 cars a month every month to only selling 4 or 5. Why? I did not believe in what I was selling. I did not want someone to spend their hard earned money on something I knew would give them trouble. I did not believe in what I was selling and I ended up broke! In no time I went from eating filet mignon to ramen noodles.

How To Create The Right Attitude

If you are going to become successful in sales you must first sell a product or service you believe in. If you do not believe in the product or service you are selling you will not become successful, you will become broke. Believe me. So, if you are in car sales and do not believe in the brand you are selling then quit and find a dealership that sells the brand you believe in, and sell it instead. Let's say it is Ford you are selling but you, for whatever reason do not like Ford, but love their competition Chevrolet, then for God's sake, sell Chevrolet. If you are selling a multi-level marketing product/business and do not believe in it then stop selling (or trying to sell it) and sell the one you do believe in. There are thousands of them out there and several of them are great companies to work for and will pay you handsomely in return. I know because I have several friends that do it.

To become successful you must have the right attitude about your product. You have to believe in your product. You have to believe in what it says, what it does, what it stands for. You must believe in it if you want to achieve in it. But, just believing in it isn't enough. Because the real question is, how much do you believe in the product you sell? This is the question you need to ask yourself. Because your depth of conviction will be the determining factor if you close that difficult customer who is on the fence between you and your competition.

So, how do you transform a belief that may be mediocre about your product to a deep internal unstoppable conviction of a belief? A belief so strong that it will cause you to sell to practically anyone anywhere? I am about to give you a simple and extremely powerful exercise I learned from a very successful salesman to do just that. First, I want you to sit down somewhere comfortable, grab a pen and a piece of paper, and take a few minutes and write down why your product or service is so great. I mean really think about why it is worth selling and why you believe your customers deserve it. Think of everything you can. Does it save them time? Does it save them money? Does it have great reviews? Does it do what it is supposed to do better than the competition? Is it the best tasting? The longest lasting? The lowest price? Will it give the best rate of return? Why do you believe in your product or service?

Remember, a belief is only a thought that has been reinforced. Reinforce your belief on why your customer would benefit from your product. Continue writing down as many positive things as possible about what you sell and the company you sell it for. I want you to believe it so much that your attitude is one that if someone does not own your product then they are truly missing out. That you are doing them a disservice by not selling it to them. Your attitude should be one that is so authentic, so genuine, and so pro your product because you believe to the core of your being that you have the best product available that if it wasn't then you wouldn't be selling it. This type of attitude will help you close more deals and make more money. And, after all, that is what you want, right?

You also must believe in yourself and your ability to sell. Sales is a field where you get paid based upon your skills. The better skill set you have the better compensation you will receive in return. Sounds nice doesn't it? I read that the best salespeople can thrive in any environment and any economy based upon one thing – THEIR ATTITUDE! If you believe in yourself you will reflect the right attitude and will learn the skills needed easily and effortlessly. Think about this for a moment. Who would learn easier? The hero who is positive, eager to make money and focuses on the opportunities available to him or her. Or, the victim who only focuses on the past, and searches for reasons why he or she was "unfairly" defeated?

One research study showed extremely positive, goal orientated, people will make about 5 million dollars more throughout their lives than someone who is negative, low energy, and non-goal orientated. Show me your attitude and I will show you the money you will earn over a life time.

You must believe in yourself, your product and/or service, and your company. If you don't then something has to change. If you do not believe in yourself then you must change that. Begin to recall all of the times in your life you did well at something, then quickly think about selling a product. Do this over and over. Because what will eventually happen is your mind will begin to associate your doing well with selling. The feelings you have of doing well at other things will neurologically attach themselves to selling and voila! You will now feel good about selling and your confidence will grow. Make sense? This is an NLP hack for creating strong positive emotions and securely attaching them to something that was once seen as scary or unfavorable. Successful salespeople use this method often because it is quick and easy. This NLP hack can also be used to attach positive emotions to a product. Get your customer to talk about something that they really like and trust and then immediately begin to talk about your product. Do this a few times and you will begin to link those good positive feelings to your product. This is what advertisers do in commercials every day and it works.

You should also use the same technique you previously used to create the unstoppable conviction belief. Write down a list of all the things you like about yourself and why you would be great at sales. It could be because you are honest, a smooth talker, have a great attitude, want to become financially independent, have a nice smile, people like you, you are a great listener, or you just truly want the best for others. Write it all down. Then focus on the list and feel good about it. This is your list. This is why you will be a great and successful salesperson.

One of the great thing about sells is that success in sales can be taught. Everything for that matter can be taught. You were taught how to ride a bike and drive a car weren't you? And, they both seemed a little daunting and scary at first didn't they? Now, you can do both without even thinking about it. Why? Because your attitude, your belief in your abilities to perform those actions are positive. Get your attitude right and your finances will follow.

Remember in life there are things you cannot control but your attitude is not one of them.

CHAPTER 2

UNSTOPPABLE MOTIVATION

"Whatever you do, be the best at it"

Motivation

What is motivation? According to Oxford Dictionaries motivation is, "The reason one has for acting or behaving in a particular way" or simply put, your motive for taking action in a given situation. I believe in simplification because the simpler things are the easier they are to learn. So I'm going to make this simple and sweet. Your motivation comes from your motives, or reasons why, you want to accomplish a particular goal. The motives are the fuel for you to do what you do. For example, some people choose to become successful and wealthy to stay away from poverty. For others it is to keep up with the Jones's and still for others it is about leaving a legacy behind after they exit this world. But regardless of your why, you must remember one thing if you want to accomplish your goals and achieve success, your why has to be bigger than your how.

You have to clearly and unwaveringly know why you want to be in a relationship with a particular person if you want that relationship to succeed. You have to clearly and unwaveringly know why you want to work for a particular company if you want to succeed within that company. You have to clearly and unwaveringly know why you want to be a salesperson if you want to be a successful salesperson. You have to clearly and unwaveringly know why you want to be successful in sales if you want to become successful in sales. If you do not have a clear picture of what you want to achieve then you will not know when you have achieved it or how to achieve it. Does that make sense? And, if you do not have strong enough reasons why you want to achieve your desired goal then you will only give up when the face of adversity rears its ugly head. Just like so many others before you. The road to success is littered with those who had good intentions but lacked strong reasons.

Average

If your why is not bigger than your how then you will only become like the majority of people walking around the world today, average. What is average? The average person is someone who at one point in their lives had great goals and aspirations. They wanted more for themselves. They wanted more for others. They saw themselves living in the huge house on the beach with their floor to ceiling bedroom windows overlooking the beautiful ocean that allowed the light from the breathtaking sunrise pour in every morning. Helping countless others change their lives with the product and services they eagerly sold. But somewhere along the way they gave up and settled for the status quo or "average". They chose the safe road with minimal risk and minimal reward. They live in the average house in the average neighborhood. Drive the average car that gets average gas mileage. They have the average thought pattern that in return returns average results. Most people are ok with being average and that is ok, for them. But not for you and me.

You see, you, like me, will not settle for average. While 80% of people will quit and give up on their goals and dreams either midway, at the end, or even before it was actually attempted, the other 20% of us will have every fiber of our being energized and programmed with only one thing in mind. To achieve! To achieve the goal that has been clearly defined in our mind. To overcome any obstacle that gets in our way. And like a heat seeking missile we will find our target. Failure is not an option we choose to see as an option.

80/20 Rule

Have you heard of Pareto's law? If not no worries because I will briefly inform you of this Universal law that applies to just about everything in life. Pareto's Law, or principle, or rule or whatever you want to call it, was named after Italian economist Vilfredo Pareto who discovered the law in the late 1800's. He discovered the "principle" or "law", if you will, by first observing that 20% of the peapods in his garden produced 80% of the peas. This prompted him to do further research to see if this bizarre phenomenon went further than his own backyard. Pareto researched and discovered that at that time in Italy 80% of the land was owned by 20% of the people. This finding further prompted Pareto to investigate even further. So he soon began to gather information and research other countries and carrying out surveys and see if the principle he discovered was

Universal or if it was only confined to his home country. To his surprise he found that the distribution of property in his own country applied to other countries as well. 20% of the people owned 80% of the land. Thus the 80/20 rule was born.

You see, this was a monster of a discovery because it can and has been applied to all areas of life with mind blowing results. Because of it, the time it takes to find solutions to problems has significantly decreased and achievements have been made at an accelerated pace. The world as we know it has been simplified. We now know, and research has confirmed, that 80% of the sales are made by 20% of the salesmen. 80% of your products are purchased by 20% of your clients. 20% of your products are purchased 80% of the time. 80% of problems can be attributed to 20% of causes. There will be 80% of the things about your job, body, and spouse etc. that you like and 20% about those things you do not like. There will also be 80% of the population that let things happen to them while only 20% of the people that make things happen, which is again, why 20% of the salespeople earn 80% the money and why 20% of the population own 80% of the land

3 Ways To Apply The 80/20 Rule To Create Success:

Focus on the problem 20% of the time and the solution 80% of the time

Know and thoroughly understand the 20% of products your company sells 80% of the time

Ask the 20% of sales superstars at your company that out sell the other 80%, what they do differently

Knowledge Isn't Power

I'm sure you have heard the statement that "knowledge is power". Well, I'm here to tell you that statement is wrong. Knowledge isn't power, applied knowledge is power. You see, if you do not do anything with the knowledge you have then it doesn't do you, or anyone else for that matter, any good. I'm sure you can think of someone right now who is blessed with an incredible amount of knowledge in a certain area or field, but takes no action. Their understanding on the subject is mind blowing and you know that if they applied their knowledge they could either change lives, make a fortune, or cure cancer, but they have no drive. They sit around wasting the day away. Then the day turns into a week. Then the month. Until eventually their entire life is wasted. It's sad. And why do they do this? Because they lack motivation. Without motivation, you will not take action.

For instance, if you are overweight and do not take action to change it, then guess what? You will stay overweight. If you are broke and do not take action to change it, then guess what? Exactly. You will stay broke. You can read this book over and over again and learn the most powerful sales techniques in the world, but if you do not apply them, then what? Exactly. They will not do you any good, will they? You must take action now if you want a change now. If you want to become successful now then you must take action now! The sooner you take action and apply what you are learning the sooner you will become successful. The sooner you become successful the sooner you can help others to become successful. And the sooner you become successful the happier you and your family will be.

How to Get Motivated

Before you begin to learn how to become an unstoppable motivation machine that accomplishes every goal in its path with precision and ease, let's first discover the three biggest factors that kill motivation. Because once you become aware of the poison that can kill your dreams you can successfully avoid them.

The number one killer of motivation and dreams is, not believing in yourself. We discussed this in the first chapter of this book on Attitude. Not having faith in yourself or your abilities is like trying to live without breathing. Just as you must breathe in order to live, you must believe in yourself in order to succeed. If you do not believe in yourself it will surely shine through to all of your customers. If you do not believe in yourself then why should they? Not believing in yourself will suffocate your dreams.

The second biggest killer is not setting goals. You must, must, must, and I can't emphasize this enough, you must set goals. There have been so many people that have landed in the average part of town because of not setting goals. If you do not know what you want or where you want to be then how will you know what to work for or when you have arrived? Not setting goals will cause you to run out of gas and leave you stranded somewhere on the road before you reach the city of success.

The third killer is trying to be perfect and comparing yourself to others. Remember the person or company you are comparing yourself to had to begin somewhere. They had to start just like you. They also had their own unique set of struggles to overcome to get where they are. The only person you have to be better than is the person you were yesterday.

Now, how do you get motivated? Pay close attention because I am about to share with you the most powerful method I've found to getting and staying motivated that is used by the most powerful people in the world. If they are using it to achieve success then shouldn't you? The power is in its simplicity. It is by knowing exactly what your desired goal is and why you want it. That simple. I will say it again. Know exactly what you want and why you want it. If you do not have a clear, and I mean crystal clear understanding of what it is you want and a list of strong reasons (motives) why you want it, then you are setting yourself up for failure. This is why powerful and successful people are so successful. Because they know exactly what they want and why they want it.

If you said you want more money and someone gave you a dollar guess what? You just received more money. If you said you want to get in shape and drop weight and you dropped one ounce then guess what? You dropped weight. You have to be crystal clear on the goal you want to achieve. If you do not know what you want to achieve then you will achieve something else. So, let's get S.M.A.R.T. about motivation.

S.M.A.R.T. goals are used by every successful company and person in existence today, which is why you should begin to use it too. It was created by George Doran, Arthur Miller, and James Cunningham to provide a simple framework to follow to successfully achieve a specific goal more effectively. Since its creation in 1981 it has been utilized by millions to transform their goals into reality, quickly and easily. Here is a breakdown of what S.M.A.R.T stands for.

S - **Simple/Specific** Keep your goal simple and focused, rather than wordy and vague. Be very specific about the outcome you want and why you want it. Give as many reasons as possible of why you need to achieve the goal.

M – **Measurable** How will you know when your goal has been reached? What will be different? How will you measure it? By measuring your goal you will be able to see the progress along the way. And, at each measureable point celebrate the progress. This will release endorphins in the brain (the happy drug) and create even more excitement and motivation to propel you forward in achieving your goal.

A – Attractive Does the goal inspire you? Is it exciting enough to keep you enthusiastic in both the long and short term? Because if the goal is not attractive when times get tough you will just give up. Make this goal mouth watering. Make it so attractive that every time you think about it you feel a smile spread across your face and you get that "I can take over the world" look on your face. The more attractive it is the more motivated you will be to achieve it.

R – Real The goal must be achievable. Can it actually be achieved? Has someone done this before? Setting your goals high and shooting for the stars is one thing but setting a goal that is unattainable is another. It will only set yourself up for failure. Be real with yourself and the rest will fall into place.

T – Timed You must put a date on the goal is to be achieved. If not the goal is only a dream. 100% of the people in the world dream but, unfortunately, only 20% of those people will accomplish their dreams. Why? Because they put a "Date to be Achieved" on their dream and take action to achieve it. If you do not put a date on it you will only make excuses of why you haven't achieved it yet, thus putting yourself in with the other 80% of the perpetual dreamers in the world.

Pleasure and Pain

The two elements that determine why and when we take action are pleasure and pain. We will do what we need to do to avoid pain and gain pleasure. Sales superstars know this and specialize in using this powerful information to their advantage to not only motivate themselves but to also motivate their customers to make a decision. I will discuss more about how they use it to motivate their customer to make a decision later in the book, but for now we will focus on using it to motivate you to become more successful in sales.

Salespeople know that by making a certain amount of cold calls they will eventually make a sale and earn a commission, which is pleasure. However, most salespeople associate more pain with making those calls. Why? You see, rather than focusing on the pleasure of gaining a sale (and a commission) they let their ego step in the way and focus on the pain of hearing "no" which is rejection. And average salespeople do not like rejection. Sales superstars know it is part of the process of becoming a superstar and learn from it. But, average salespeople avoid it at all costs. They avoid the pain of being rejected by making excuses for their inactions such as; "Well, I will call them after I have my cup of coffee." "Well, I'm sure they are busy now, so I will call them after lunch." "I have to check my emails, so when I'm done with this, I will make the calls." "Well, they are probably getting ready to leave the office by now, so I will just call them tomorrow." This way, they are able to put off making the calls and not having to deal with any form of rejection and keeping their precious ego intact.

How do you become a sales superstar? Easy. Instead of associating pain with a task, like average salespeople, associate pain with not taking action on the task and pleasure with taking action. That is what sales superstars do. How can you do this? It is quite simple really. Make yourself a list of the reasons why it would be pleasurable for you to take action. Make this list as long as you can. Put everything you can think of that will give you pleasure on this list. I want you to get excited when you look at this list.

Some of the things on the list might be, "It will be over when I finish." "It will guarantee that I keep my job." "It will guarantee a sale." "It will guarantee that my commission check is bigger than last week's." "It will allow me to take my wife out on a nice date." "It will allow me to pay my kid's college tuition." "I will become the top salesperson in the company." "My confidence grows more and more with each phone call I make." "I get better and better with each person I speak to."

Afterward, make a list of why it would cause pain not to take action. "You will feel bad about yourself." "Your commission check will suck." "You cannot take your wife out on the nice date that she truly deserves." "Your kid will have to quit school." "You will feel like a failure." Associate as much pain with not taking action as you possibly can and associate as much pleasure as you possibly can with taking action and your motivation will be unstoppable.

Avoid Procrastination

Procrastination is like being on a sinking ship out in the middle of the ocean. You will feel hopeless and end up on the bottom unless you take action. Now, let's take a quick look at the number one reason people procrastinate, so we can avoid it. The number one reason people procrastinate, contrary to popular belief, is not because of lack of motivation, it is because of overwhelm. Instead of breaking a problem or situation down into smaller manageable parts, most people will look at the overall picture, feel an enormous amount of pressure overcome them, and just stop in their tracks. They simply become frustrated, "overwhelmed", and put off doing whatever it is that needs to be done.

While I was selling cars I had a co-worker that was normally jovial and cracking jokes with everyone in sight but on this one particular day she had nothing to say and had this look of "lost" on her little face. I pulled her to the side and asked her what was going on because she was not her usual self. She was almost in tears talking to me and told me that she was feeling overwhelmed and had so much to do but didn't know where to start and that, "She just couldn't do it." I calmed her down and asked her what was she "overwhelmed" about and she replied, "The lease on my apartment is about to be up. I have to move but I'm not sure where. I have to buy furniture. I do not know if the apartments close to work are in a good area with little to no crime and I need to find a gym."

After breaking down each element of her "overwhelming" situation we easily found a solution. The only piece of furniture she needed to purchase was a new couch, which was going to be fun to shop for. We made a few phone calls and discovered that both apartment options near work were great and safe and that there was a 24 hour gym close by. Within a matter of minutes she went from feeling overwhelmed and frustrated to feeling light and carefree. Why? Because when you look at everything that needs to get done and think that it all has to get done now, it is too much for the brain to process and you simply shut down all of your rational capacities. But, when you breakdown or "chunk" the pieces of the situation into smaller manageable sections they become easier to handle, less "overwhelming" and a solution can be found.

The same process holds true for making those dreaded cold calls or follow up calls. If you look at all of the calls you need to make and think, "man, I'm never going to get these done today, there's so many of them." It's easy to procrastinate due to the "overwhelming" number of them but if you break the list down and make an agreement with yourself to make, say five calls, then take a brief break to regroup, and then start again, then it will be easier and more manageable for you.

Procrastination only compounds problems causing them to look hopeless. Take immediate action by breaking down the situation into smaller manageable pieces, feel the pressure melt away, and get started. I want you, if you are a procrastinator, to link major pain to procrastination and extreme pleasure to taking immediate action. The more things you do promptly, the easier everything else will be. And the more you do this the more of a habit it becomes until it is simply second nature for you, just like brushing your teeth before bed.

Monitor The Progress You Are Making And Reward Yourself

This is a sure way to increase motivation. If you are in sales, then you should love progress. You see, the more progress you make, the bigger your paychecks become. More progress equals more money, so I would suggest you celebrate each time you get a paycheck that is bigger than the last.

How and what do you monitor? After each interaction with a customer take a few minutes and log down what happened. What type of customer where they? Were they more internal (valued their opinions more) or external (valued others opinions more)? Were they towards (made decisions based on achieving and gaining) or away from (motivated to stay away from something negative) values? Did you have rapport with this person? What objections did you encounter? Did you close the sale? After writing this down after each customer you will begin to see what type of customers you work easily with and what type of customer you need to improve on. It will tell you if you are strong at gaining rapport with others or weak. It will show you what objections you personally receive and allow you to prepare for them so you can overcome them with ease. It will also reveal your closing percentage, which is huge because it is a direct reflection to your paycheck.

So after you have this information monitor it every week and look for any improvements you may have. Successful people keep records of their performance. It keeps them sharp and motivated. If you have improvements, then celebrate them. Reward yourself for doing well. There is nothing wrong with rewarding yourself. Now, I'm not saying to go out and blow your entire paycheck. What I am saying is treat yourself to something that will make you feel good.

Think about it like this, a child feels good when they are rewarded, right? Well, you were a child once and I'm sure you still feel good when you get rewarded. For this reason, reward yourself, you deserve it. If you do not like rewarding yourself, then reward someone else. Make someone else feel good. It is scientifically proven that if you do something good for someone else, you will have the same feeling, as though you were the recipient of the good deed. The more you give, the more you will receive. Don't believe me? Try it for yourself. The main objective here is to celebrate your progress.

Accountability

Accountability is the pathway to goal achievement. Accountability is one of the specific reasons many people join Alcoholics Anonymous and are able to overcome their addiction. Accountability is also one of the reasons so many people hire sales coaches, life coaches, and athletic coaches. Coaches help their clients determine their goals, create an action plan to achieve them, and then hold them accountable during the process.

If you are serious about becoming successful in sales and want to increase your income then partner with another salesperson, friend, spouse, or hire a sales coach and inform them of what your goal is. Then have them hold you accountable for achieving it. Have them check in with you several times a month. Have them ask you, "How your sales are going?" "What areas you can improve in?" "Are you on target to achieving your goal?" If you are held accountable for the actions you take then the actions you take will achieve your goal. If you are held accountable you will continue to stay motivated to do the right thing at the right time which in turn will only increase your commission check.

This powerful technique is implemented by sales superstars all over the world and in every industry to substantially increase their income. They have made a public declaration that they will achieve a certain goal and they do not want to let anyone down. Why is the accountability partner so crucial? Because you might be okay with not hitting your goal for the month or even the year and letting yourself down. But letting someone else down is a whole different ballgame. The moment you let someone in on your goal and make it publicly known is the moment you set yourself apart from the average salesperson. Set goals, have someone hold you accountable, become successful. The End!

Body Language

Body language has more to do with your feelings than you may realize. Studies prove that a two-minute power pose (a pose that makes you feel powerful) has been proven to increase confidence and your natural testosterone output by 25%.

Think about this for a moment. How does someone who is depressed, stand? How does this person look? How does this person breathe? Where are their shoulders? How do they speak? Now, make your body replicate this. Next, try to feel motivated while maintaining this posture and breathing pattern. You cannot do it. It is impossible. Your brain will not let you. Your body is sending signals to your brain that you are depressed, so your genie has to create this state for you.

Now, I want you to think about someone who is completely confident and motivated. How do they stand? How do they breathe? How do they look? Where are their shoulders? I want you to take on this posture. How do you feel now? Take that feeling and double it. Notice in your body where you feel this energy is starting and where it is moving, because energy is always moving, it cannot stay in one place, and it always moves in a circular motion. Observe which way the energy is rotating and increase the speed, feeling, and magnitude until you have doubled it. Pretty cool, huh? Now, double it again. You can now create this feeling at will by repeating what you just learned. This is a little NLP technique used by top sales professionals to increase their confidence quickly and easily. Now, like them, so can you.

Your state of mind and the way you feel about what you do you can increase your pleasure and productivity. Think about when you first started dating your significant other. Remember in the beginning, how much you used to do to make that person happy and you enjoyed doing it? And remember how you would go above and beyond to see them happy? And remember how just hearing that person's name made you excited and put you in a better mood?

And when you are in a better mood, everything else just seems to flow to you perfectly and effortlessly, doesn't it? And if you are in a better mood, if things did not go quite right, it still did not seem that bad, did they? That is the power of enjoying what you do. If you begin to look for reasons why you enjoy what you do, you will create a better state of mind for what it is you do.

Remember the 80/20 rule? I talk about this often. There will be 80% of things about your job, your body, your relationship, your home, everything, which you enjoy, and 20% about those things you do not enjoy. Whatever you focus your attention on is going to determine your emotional state. If you focus on the 20% of things you do not like, then how do you think you are going to feel? If you focus on the 80% of things you do enjoy, how do you think you will feel then? Which state do you think will enable you to sell more products? Which state do you think you should be in to get the most referrals? Which state do you think the top salespeople in your industry are in when they are with their clients?

If you are complaining to a prospect about your company and the internal problems it has and how it could run so much more efficiently, then I feel pretty certain that your prospect will not send you any referrals. I mean, think about it, why should they want to send a friend to you that could potentially have an issue with the service or product? That would not make them a good friend, would it? It would only discredit their credibility and they do not want that. You will be lucky to even get the deal you are working on.

Focus

What you focus your attention on you will see and receive in return. If you focus on not being broke or "I don't want to be broke," then you are actually focusing on being broke. How? Because you constantly focus on what broke looks like and what it feels like and tell yourself you don't want that. The problem with that is your brain is very literal and it does not compute the word "don't". For example. Don't think of a piping hot pizza being pulled out of the oven at your favorite pizza restaurant. Now, did you think about the piping hot pizza? How about the oven it was being pulled out of? Or how about your favorite pizza restaurant? You see, you brain has to first see what you "don't" want it to see. So to correct this way of thinking and improve your success and what you truly want to achieve in life practice saying and focusing on what you want. Instead of "not being broke", how about "being wealthy"? Instead of saying, "I don't want to blow this sale", say, "This sale is going to be easy and the customer will enjoy giving me their business, now."

What you focus on in life you will see. 80% of the people focus on the problem while 20% of people focus on the solution. Take a look around the room for five quick seconds right now and notice all the things you see that are brown. Perfect. Now say out loud everything you noticed that was red. Exactly. You probably didn't notice many things red or any at all did you. Now look around the room and notice all the red things in the room. You see, you will find whatever you focus you attention on. So, focus on success, opportunity, improvement, fun, happiness, balance. Focus on the things you want in life not on what you don't want.

CHAPTER 3

INSTANTLY BUILD RAPPORT

"No one can make you feel inferior without your consent."

Eleanor Roosevelt

Rapport

To become a master communicator and close more deals than you ever thought possible, you must learn how to create rapport. What is rapport? Have you ever met someone and you just "hit it off?" That is rapport. Rapport is having a connection between two or more people. The basic definition of rapport is, "A relationship marked by mutual understanding and trust." You must understand that when you have rapport, whether it is with one person or with a group of people, you instantly possess unlimited power to achieve a desired outcome.

This outcome could be as grand as the, "I have a dream" speech given by Dr. Martin Luther King Jr., which was the defining moment in the civil rights movement, or closing a sale with a customer who is interested in your product. Either way, with rapport great things can be achieved, but without it, simple tasks can seem impossible to accomplish.

You see, without rapport there is no trust. And trust is an extremely powerful motivating factor for others to take action. Friends trust one another and friends are the ones you can always trust to be there in a time of need. If you are in a bind and need some help, who do you call? A friend. If you want to go off and have a night out, who do you call? A friend. If you have an issue and need some advice, who do you call? A friend. You trust that friend to be there and give you what you need when you need it; therefore, you are obligated to reciprocate.

This is one of the reasons why rapport is so important, because it builds trust and when someone trusts you, they feel obligated to take action for you. Think about this for a moment also. Who would you rather buy from, a friend or a salesman? And which friend would you rather take advice from, the friend who is confident and knowledgeable of the subject being discussed or the friend who is unsure of himself and is clueless about the subject you are talking about? Sales are the same way. You would rather buy from a friend and you would rather take advice from the friend who is knowledgeable of the subject being discussed. To easily close more deals and earn more money you need to become the customer's friend who is knowledgeable of the product being sold. That simple.

When you instantly build rapport and the prospect "likes" you, feels comfortable in your presence, and feels that you have the knowledge and expertise on the subject being discussed, they will give you the time to earn their business. In fact, they will be more than happy to give you the time to earn their business. Why? Because other salespeople are simply not like you. They are not as good as you. They are not as "cool" as you. They do not feel like the other salespeople out there are their friend. I have closed sale after sale from having great rapport with my customers. Time and time again I have heard, "You are not like other salespeople. You are different. I like you." And after the sale have invited me to dinner or out to have a drink. To this day I still have several customers that I still meet up with for dinner or a drink.

Let's go a little deeper in the human psyche for just a moment. People are internally wired to like people who are the same as them. It is the compare and contrast mechanism in our nervous system at work. If someone is similar to you then you know what to expect from them, to a certain degree, and that puts them in your comfort zone. But, if they are different than you then you may not know what to expect from them, to a certain degree, and that puts them out of your comfort zone. Here are a few examples. If someone is honest, they do not like someone who is dishonest. If a person is loyal, then they will not like disloyalty? If someone is clean and tidy then they will not like someone who is messy and unorganized? Let me ask you a question. If a person is an adrenaline junkie and makes plans in the moment, chances are they are not going to like the couch potato that makes sure their day is always planned out from the time they wake up till the time they go to bed, are they? No. Exactly.

Take John for instance. John is an IT consultant in his mid-twenties who grew up in South Georgia as an only child. He is well mannered, educated, trustworthy, and would not harm a fly. John is also a huge comic book and video game junkie, and every second of his spare time is consumed with his games and comic books.

John has a girlfriend named Sarah. And when John and Sarah first began dating, she wanted him to have more friends. John was introverted and friends were hard to come by for him but, his girlfriend Sarah on the other hand was the complete opposite. She was a social butterfly and had a ton of friends. She loved going out to social events and double dates so she introduced John to some of her girlfriend's husbands, hoping they would hit it off and become friends themselves.

One night, while at a party with his girlfriend and all of her girlfriends and their husbands, John tried his best to fit in and make friends with them. He walked over, shyly, and as he awkwardly stood there for a moment until he finally built up enough confidence and began to strike up a conversation with the group of husbands. He began to talk about his character from his favorite video game. The group of husbands all looked puzzled as they stared at John for a moment because they had no idea what he was talking about. None of them played video games. So, they just turned back around huddled in their little circle and picked up their conversation right where they left off, leaving John out in the cold.

You see, they are all junkies too, but unfortunately for John, they were adrenaline junkies that loved extreme sports. They were into things such as skydiving, racing, windsurfing, etc. As previously mentioned, John was also shy and it was obvious in his demeanor, whereas the group of husbands were extremely extroverted and confident. This extreme difference in the types of people wasn't the reason John was unable to make friends with them, it was how he tried to go about it.

Rapport within a group is usually why the group acts similar to one another. They have similar traits or characteristics, and when an outsider tries to infiltrate the circle (become friends) and has similar traits or characteristics (posture, movements, tonality, sentence structure, similar experiences) as the current members, they are more likely to be invited to join. However, on the other hand, if the person is completely different, as in John's case, they will quickly be shunned from the group.

A very powerful covert way to gain rapport and control within a new group of people or a business deal, with more than one person you are selling to, is by being aware of who the decision maker is and matching their speaking pattern, voice tone, rhythm, inflections, and metaphors. We will discuss this in detail soon. If John had known this secret covert technique and applied it, the likelihood of him gaining acceptance into the group would have drastically improved if not guaranteeing him a position.

You have to keep in mind, people like those who are like themselves or they like those who possess the qualities they would like to possess. Building rapport is the easiest way to get others to like you. There are several avenues one can take to accomplish the goal of building rapport, but to build it instantly and easily, you want to match and mirror. The two terms, match and mirror are self-explanatory. You want to match what the person you want to build rapport with is doing (copy body movement in the same direction) or mirror it. (Copy but only in the opposite direction) Think of it as looking in a mirror.

Most studies illustrate that the communication that takes place between people essentially breaks down into three areas:

Words: 7%

Tonality: 38%

Physiology: 55%

You see it is not what we say, but how we say it. Words only account for 7% of our communication while the other whopping 93% of it is tonality and physiology. This is why understanding and mastering of the art of rapport is crucial to your pursuit of success in sales and is why all top salespeople set out to master it. Knowing the right words to say is one thing but knowing how to say it and using proper body language is the key to closing more deals. The techniques you are about to learn to build rapport are the same techniques being taught by other top sales trainers in the world. These powerful techniques will make the process of building rapport so simple that you will wonder how everyone else does not know them. But the question isn't why doesn't everyone else know them, the real question is how many more deals will you close from these newly discovered techniques?

Areas To Match Or Mirror

Match Their Modality - Modality in NLP (Neuro Linguistic Programming) refers to the way a person communicates. People predominately communicate in one of these three ways or a combination of all of them; visual (seeing), auditory (hearing), or kinesthetic (feeling).

Once you notice the customer's primary communication pattern, use it to communicate with them. If they use words such as see, show, foggy, clear, vivid, bright, dim, close, etc., (visual words), then this person's main representational pattern for communication is visual. Representational pattern is how the person represents or perceives and communicates the world in which they live in. So, you should use the same words back to them when describing and communicating.

If the person uses words such as crystal clear, loud, quiet, resonate, rings a bell, tunes in, do you hear what I'm saying, (hearing words) etc., then they are more auditory. If they use words such as rough, smooth, this is a tough situation, smooth as glass, grasp, slip, fall into, deep, shallow, (feeling words), then they are kinesthetically driven communicators. Use similar representational words back to the person to build rapport. Remember, keep things simple.

List of The Representational Systems and Their Words or Phrases:

Visual - See, look, bright, clear, foggy, hazy, view, focused, reveal, imagine, illuminate, picture, sight for sore eyes, naked eye, bird's eye view, take a peek, paint a picture, short sighted, clear cut, catch a glimpse, dim view, draw me a diagram, beyond a shadow of a doubt, hazy idea, get a perspective on, in person, a horse of a different color, looks like, in light of, mental image, clear view, tunnel vision, under your nose, showing off.

Auditory - Hear, sound, tell, melody, roar, silence, listen, resonate, harmonize, deaf, squeak, music, rhythm, loud, quiet, soft, rattle, tone, harmony, in tune, out of tune, tuned in, tuned out, overtone, rings a bell, on another note, loud and clear, purrs like a kitten, voiced and opinion, give me an ear, blabber mouth, afterthought, give an account of, hold your tongue, idle talk, earful, describe in detail, manner of speaking, pay attention to, power of speech.

Kinesthetic – Grasp, scrape, solid, smooth, pull, hard, feel, unfeeling, touch, concrete, comfortable, slippery, clasp, rock heavy, lift, light, push, sink, uphill, pull some strings, smooth operator, get a handle on, get in touch with, sharp as a tack, make contact, boils down to, all washed up, get a load of this, chip off the old block, control yourself, get the drift, hand in hand, hot head, keep your hat on, lay your cards on the table, slipped my mind, start from scratch, pain in the neck.

Statistics suggest that the majority of people are predominately visual (60%), while auditory and kinesthetic are 20% each.

Match And Mirror Their Physiology - When we copy the physical movements of another individual such as facial expressions, blinking rate, posture, hand movements, etc., it subconsciously sends signals to that person that we are alike, and remember, people like those who are like themselves. If you notice that the prospect sits back in their chair and crosses their leg, take a few moments and then you do the same thing. If the client uses their hands to talk, then use your hands to talk.

However, do not do it to the point where it is obvious what you are doing. You want to make it look natural. Make it look like this is how you communicate. If they blink, then wait a few moments and you blink. You will be surprised at how powerful this part of matching and mirroring really is.

Match Their Voice And Language - You do this by matching the volume, tone, and tempo of the other person's speech. If they speak in a slow manner, you speak in a slow manner. If they speak at an elevated volume, then you speak at an elevated volume. And if they speak quiet and slowly, then you do the same. You get the idea by now, right?

You can also use the same words they use, which will further reinforce rapport. If they say something to the effect of, "I am looking for the perfect beach home with the most beautiful view of the ocean," then you repeat it back to them. Don't change their words. Do not say, "Wow, you're in luck. I have the best beach house with a pleasing view available," instead say, "You are looking for the perfect beach home with the most beautiful view? Mrs. Jones, I have the perfect beach home right down the road with a beautiful view of the ocean. Let's go have a look at it."

Match Their Breathing - People breathe from either high in the chest, the middle of the chest, or from their belly. Notice where the other person is breathing from.

Also notice at the rate and depth at which they are taking their breaths and match it. Are they breathing shallow or deep, high in the chest or low in the belly? Be observant. The more you practice the easier it will become for you.

This is a subtle method that can have a very high impact on building rapport. It will put you in sync with the other person and have you able to understand their mood on a deeper level. You can also match their breathing with tapping. You can tap your finger on your arm if they are folded or lightly on the desk if you are sitting at one. Or you could even bob your foot up and down to the tempo of their chest rising and falling, to match their breathing.

Match The Size Of Information They Use - Most people can only understand the amount of information given to them at the same rate they speak it. Understanding this is an absolute must if you want the other person to understand you better, like you more, and drastically improve your chances of closing the sale.

If the other person speaks very slowly and uses five words before the break, or slight pause, in their sentence and repeats this cadence, then you do the same. This is because if you speak fast and use twenty words before taking a breath while your client only uses five words, you will completely lose the client and can plan on them going somewhere else to speak to someone else who they can understand and relate to. Speak at their rate and they will buy at yours.

Match Their Common Experience - Again, people like those who are like themselves. If someone tells you that they are an adrenaline junkie and love sky diving and such, then do not tell them about your knitting hobby and butterfly collection. This will only bore them and will not build rapport.

Talk about similar subjects and experiences, as this is a quick way to get someone smiling with you and instantly feeling comfortable. The reason is they do not feel like they have to tell their entire life story to a stranger. They are already talking with someone like them, someone who already understands them.

Note: Pace yourself while copying their actions. People do not like to be mimicked and made fun of, so you have to be careful with matching and mirroring. Do not replicate every movement right after they make it, it will look awkward and have the opposite effect on the person you are speaking with. Give it a few seconds and casually copy the movements.

Do not overdo the matching and mirroring. Too much of anything is a bad thing. Once you notice you have achieved your goal of rapport, then you are good and there is no need to continue the process of matching and mirroring body language the entire time. The only time you want to start again is if you notice you two fell out of rapport. For instance, if a subject was touched on and there were two completely opposing views and the prospect is agitated, quickly change subject and begin building rapport again.

Pacing and Leading

Pacing and leading is a great way to see if you are in rapport with someone. Notice if they begin to change their communication when you change yours. Speed up the rate at which you speak or slow it down and see if the other person follows your lead. If you notice the other person following your rate of speech, then you are leading them and have powerful rapport. If you notice that while at dinner, someone tilts their glass and you then do the same thing, they are leading you and have subconsciously built a strong rapport with you. Pacing is following the leader.

Calibration is another way to test if the person is in rapport with you. Calibration is being aware of the other person's reactions to your communication. By becoming aware of how they react, you can begin to change your communication with them accordingly. For instance, if you brought up a subject that has caused their pupils to grow smaller, their nostrils to flair out, and a slight redness arises in their face, then it would be a good idea to change the subject and not bring that one back up. A professional salesperson is always aware of their prospect's mood at all times.

Make the Process Simple

I can't say this enough, do not over complicate the process. Use the same metaphors the person you are speaking to uses. It is much easier for a person to understand you in a shorter amount of time by using the same metaphors they use than it would be for them having to decipher your metaphors. If the person you are speaking to is a very formal type and uses a wide range of exceptional vocabulary words, then you do the same. If the person is laid back and uses words such as cool, awesome, fun, then you do the same. If you keep it simple, it will be a quick and easy path to rapport.

Think about someone who you just "hit it off" with the very first time you met them. If you remember correctly I'm sure you had several things in common with them. Two of those things being, speaking with similar metaphors and having similar physiological characteristics. And because of this, whether you were consciously aware of it or not, it made the encounter enjoyable. Have you ever met someone and who you did not gain rapport and just "hit it off" because they either spoke completely over your head or beneath your feet? When this happens there is usually no connection there and everything just feels awkward and because of it you will want to get the engagement over as quickly as possible. Everyone involved in situations like this feel the same way.

You see, people want to enjoy their time. No one wants to deliberately have a bad time and this is what happens when you do not have rapport with someone. They do not trust you and are not going to enjoy the time spent with you. Build rapport because rapport builds "like" and "trust" and when someone likes you and trusts you, they will buy from you.

I was selling pool tables in my early twenties, when a woman came inside the store to "browse" around. While talking to her I began showing her a beautiful pool table with a lot of detailed carving in it, which I could tell she liked tremendously. After receiving all the nonverbal "tell me more" signs I began explaining the features and benefits to her. Now, early on, she told me she was "just looking", but "just looking" never stopped me from my success in sales formula – building rapport, fact finding, and trial closing, and should never stop you, if you want to be successful. If we believed everyone who said they were "just looking", we would all starve to death. By the time I finished my presentation, I was jumping up and down on the table and joking with the woman. The woman who was "just looking" ended up buying a very expensive pool table from me. While I was scheduling the delivery, she told me she had no intention of buying a pool table, but that she just felt comfortable with me trusted me and loved my enthusiasm about my product.

Customers buy when they like you and trust you. This lady was just walking around and letting her food settle before she went back to work and before she knew it, she was the proud owner of one of the best and most beautiful pool tables ever made.

Practice Makes Perfect

Practice building rapport with others around you. Practice with family and friends. Practice with strangers in a restaurant or while on a bus or plane or standing in line getting some coffee. Practice with everyone and practice often, because as you already know, practice is the path to perfection and perfection is a journey not a destination. To get very good at this very quickly, chunk it down into areas and focus on only one area at a time, for a specific amount of time.

For instance, spend a day or even a week just practicing nonverbal rapport building. Match someone's breathing or posture and body movements. Match their blinking rate, gestures, and breathing. But, when you do, do not be surprised if the person you are building rapport with comes over and begins a conversation with you, as this happens very often. Afterwards, spend some time matching a person's voice tone. Begin to notice their speaking patterns, how many words they speak before they take a brief pause and start again. Also, pay attention to the metaphors they use while speaking.

The information in this chapter is extremely powerful and life changing and once you understand this process and begin to apply it, others will ask you "Why does everyone you meet seem to like you so much?" Or, "You never seem to meet a stranger." It will also strengthen your relationships and increase your bank account.

Watch television shows or movies and begin to be aware of other people's posture and blinking patterns. Notice if the dialogue being used is mostly a visual, auditory, or a kinesthetic representational pattern. The more you practice this, the easier it will become. It will become so easy that you will eventually not even think about what to look for at all. You will just know.

It works just like math problems, when you first learned how to count and add, you had to think about it, but now you already know how to count and add without thinking about it, you just do it, don't you? The process of instantly building rapport is the same way. Practice this and you will absolutely begin to see a change in the way other people interact with you.

CHAPTER 4

STRATEGIC FACT FINDING

"Ask the right questions at the right time and you will get the right outcome"

Understanding Fact Finding

Fact finding can be one of the most enjoyable and exciting parts of the entire sales process. Why? Because if the fact finding - investigating, qualifying or whatever label you want to give it - is done correctly, it will enable you to close more deals easily and effortlessly. After all, that is what you want right, to close more deals and earn more money?

Once you master your skill in this area, you will have customers bending over backwards to give you their business. The reason is because no other salesperson will know the powerful covert techniques you know that create a sense connection, understanding, and confidence. No other salesperson will ask the right questions at the right time and in a way that makes the customer feel as if they were buying from a friend they have known their entire life. No other salesperson will have verbally treated them so elegantly and with such class as you. And you know this to be true because if the customer had been treated in such a way before, then they wouldn't be there talking to you right now, they would be purchasing from the previous salesperson.

It is all about asking the right questions at the right time. Ask the right questions and you get the right outcome. When done correctly you will witness your customers sending you referrals on a regular basis due to being extremely grateful for the product or service your provided. You will be the salesman they purchase from for a lifetime.

A lot of salespeople have particularly weak skills at this step the sales process and do one or two things wrong. They either one, sound like they are literally interrogating the customer to death or two, have no direction with their questions at all. A top sales professional once told me that at this particular juncture of the sales process, you should turn into a private investigator.

He said, "It is your job to find out everything you need to know to provide the prospect with what they need to purchase today. If you do your investigating properly, you will close every deal. "If you know what your customer wants, why they want it, what they like about the current version they own, what they dislike about the current version they own, and anchor positive emotions to your product, then you will be a superstar in the area of investigating. If you are a superstar in this area of the sales process, then be prepared for supersized earnings."

Now, some customers have their guard up and will not give up the information you are searching for easily and that's ok because you will be prepared for it. There are several reasons for this type of behavior - they have not settled on a particular product or brand yet, they like to find out all the information on their own and then ask for your assistance, or they are not the final decision maker. Nevertheless, this type of customer has been taken advantage of by a salesman before and does not want it to happen again.

An easy way to handle this type of customer is by saying, "Before we begin anything, I have some things I would like to go over." We will soon discuss this proven covert technique, but before we get started with that, I have something I want to go over with you.

Covertly Breaking Past the Customer's Guard

Richard Bandler, in his book, "Persuasion Engineering," spoke about fact finding and he gave an example of an extremely powerful pattern to break down the guard of the customer so you can easily retrieve the information you desire. He said that if someone came into a car dealership and said,

"Well, I am here to look for a car." His response would be, "Well, I won't show you a car right now. There is something more important we need to deal with first because I don't want to sell you the wrong car, I don't want to sell you a car that you can't afford. I only want to make sure that you understand my job is to make sure that you are making the right decision. Now, I know in the past, there were times you've made the right decision, you've bought something and it's been perfect for you and you were totally satisfied and there were times where perhaps, you've bought something and then afterwards weren't satisfied. It's my job to make sure you use your best judgment. So, I want to ask you a couple of questions first."

This is an extremely powerful technique that can be used or altered to suit whatever it is you are selling; from cars to insurance, to jets, to real estate to arts and crafts. The reason it is so powerful is because it instantly conveys to the customer that you are there for them and that you have their best interest at heart. And once a customer knows that you are not like some of the other "pushy" salespeople only there to high gross a customer and then move on to the next victim, they will happily share with you what you need to know. The customer's time and money are valuable and they want to be treated as such, and rightfully so.

Another technique that will put the customer at ease and allow you to covertly gather the information needed is the, "Before we begin" technique. You can use this technique before you start fact finding or closing, it works great in both areas.

Just before you begin to ask your customer some of your fact finding questions, simply say to the customer, "Before we begin, I have some things I would like to ask you." Then you begin asking your fact finding/qualifying questions. By making this statement before you start, the customer puts their guard down. They do not feel a need to have it up because there is no threat and they will continue to stay in a relaxed and comfortable state, and before they know it, you have all the information you need to sell them the product they want to purchase.

I know some sales professionals that use this with just about every customer they speak to and receive incredible results with it. Because after all, you only need to know a handful of powerful techniques and apply them with precision to receive the desired results. The customer will not know if you used the same technique on the customer before them or not. Did you know a major league pitcher only has about five different pitches? He practices his pitches over and over again, until he has mastered them to perfection. And those five pitches that he has perfected, he will use over and over and over and collect win after win after win. While you read this powerful book and learn these powerful techniques, I want you to begin to put together your perfect pitches. Practice them over and over and over until you have perfected them with precision. Once you do this, you, like the major league pitcher, will collect win after win after win, but instead of winning baseball games, you will be winning with deals.

Wants, Needs, and Desires

Wants, needs, and desires are ultimately what you are searching for during the fact finding phase of the sales process. Their "hot buttons". Once you have discovered the customer's wants, needs, and desires, in a way that you can speak to them with a hypnotic language, which you are now learning, you will be unstoppable.

Once you know that information, you can place it in your pitch, in your close, and use it to obliterate any objection they may have. Knowing their wants, needs, and desires are the key to delivering the perfect pitch and overcoming objections. And the best time to overcome an objection is before it even starts. We will cover more on overcoming objections soon. So, how do you discover their wants, needs, and desires? Skillfully. Here are some skillful techniques to assist in understanding what you are searching for and how to get it.

<u>N.E.A.D.S.</u> is a technique that Tom Hopkins uses to find facts and it is discussed in his book, "Selling for Dummies." This technique is quite popular and used by a lot of the top sales professionals across all industries.

N What do they have NOW?

E What do they ENJOY most about what they have now?

A What would they ALTER or change about what they have now?

D Who is the final DECISION maker?

S As a professional, it's my responsibility to help them find the best SOLUTION to their needs.

If you are a car salesman and a customer comes to your dealership and is looking for a new car, following the N.E.A.D.S. technique, you would begin by finding out what they currently drive and what they enjoy about it.

You would say something to the effect of, "I noticed you drove the Mercedes SL500 in today. That is a very nice car. How long have you owned it? Then whatever answer they give, you nod and say, "Perfect." Then ask,

"So, tell me, what do you like about that car?" The reason for this question is for you to discover what they like, their "hot buttons." Once you discover their hot buttons store them to use in the sales pitch at the right time.

After you find out what they like about the current vehicle, ask them, "If you could alter or change anything about the Benz what would it be?" The reason for this question is so you will know what they are looking for in the car they are going to purchase from you. It allows you to prepare for your feature and benefit process on the car they will be purchasing from you. After this is determined, it is time to verify if they are the final decision maker for the purchase.

There is nothing worse than going through all the motions, doing everything perfectly, asking all the right questions, eliciting all the right emotions and responses, giving the perfect pitch, and then finding out that they are not the decision maker.

So, to avoid this dreadful deal stopping act from happening, all you have to do is ask. It's that simple. You ask, "Will there be anyone else involved in the buying process or transaction (whichever you feel more comfortable with)?" Or, "Well it seems you know exactly what you are looking for. Will anyone be assisting you in the decision to buy today?" Also, there is an embedded command in that one, buy today.

Embedded commands are used with incredible results and we will be discussing more of it soon. Then lastly, you will help them find the solution to their needs. This is the easy part, all you have to do is select the vehicle that meets the wants, needs and desires of your client.

What Is In It For me?

This is something that the customer or client is always thinking in the back of their mind. "What is in it for me if I buy your product or service?" "What is in it for me if I invest in your venture?" "What is in it for me if I take your course?" This is something you must always remember. If you are one of those salespeople who go on and on (I would not advise this by the way) about how great your company is and how you are number one in the industry and how you are the top producer at your company blah blah blah, the customer is going to very quickly tune you out and move on.

Sure, the customer wants to know he is dealing with a professional and that the company he is considering doing business with is reputable, but he does not want it crammed down his throat. He wants to know what is in it for him. While you are gloating about how great your company is, all he wants to know is what your great company can do for him. While you are gloating about how great you are, all he wants to know is what your great little self can do for him.

This is why you fact find. If you understand what the customer's wants, needs, and desires are, then you can show the customer what is in it for them. If you are selling a car and the customer is looking for something with ample leg room for the family and great on gas because they take a lot of long distance road trips, you would show the customer what your vehicle has to offer to satisfy those needs.

You would show him a vehicle with plenty of cabin space and great gas mileage. You would not show the customer a supped up sports car that gets ten miles to the gallon, would you? If so, you will not be in the sales business for long. You would hopefully show them what your product has to satisfy their wants, needs, and desires, not yours.

You see, people are emotional creatures. People buy based on emotions and justify with logic. So do not only tell your prospect how great your product is and that it will satisfy their wants, needs, and desires, show them. Make the customer see it, feel it, and smell it. Get all of their senses involved. The more you get your prospect's senses involved, the more likely they are to say "Yes". Find out whatever is the most important to a prospect that will make them want to purchase and give it to them.

Intonation

Get ready to learn something that will blow you away with how effective it works. By linking a different intonation pattern to the sentence structure you use, you begin to create new possibilities for the outcome of the sentence. Intonation is the voice inflections (rise, fall, or flat) at the end of a sentence. I want you to either say these next three sentences aloud so you will get a better understanding of the hypnotic power that is taking place.

Normally, when you ask a question the voice inflection rises, right? Example: "You're going to make the purchase?" But if you change the intonation, then you change the sentence. If you drop the intonation, or voice inflection at the end of the sentence, then you make the sentence a command. Example, "You're going to make the purchase!" And then you can also change it yet again by just keeping a monotone with the sentence all the way through and it will be just a statement. Example, "You're going to make the purchase."

Below is a diagram of how voice intonation is structured.

Word $\Longrightarrow$ **W**ord $\Longrightarrow$ **W**ord   **= Question**

Word $\Longrightarrow$ **W**ord $\Longrightarrow$ **W**ord   **= Statement**

Word $\Longrightarrow$ **W**ord $\Longrightarrow$ **W**ord   **= Command**

The power hidden in intonation is mind blowing. Just follow me here for a moment because once you truly understand the power that intonation possess and the results you are able to generate by applying it, you will soon be using this powerful covert technique in every conversation you have. Trust me, I know.

You see, we are all conditioned to answer a question, but when there is no question being asked, we inherently nod our heads in agreeance or simply say yes verbally. When we hear someone bark a command, we tend to act accordingly. For instance, when you were a little mischievous as a child and did something you were not supposed to do, like color on the walls, and your mom or dad yelled, "Get in here!" intonation down, which meant a command, you acted accordingly. You immediately ran to where they were.

You see, we are conditioned since childhood to follow a certain set of language patterns and once you know how to manipulate them properly, you can have others act according to what you want. You have no doubt unknowingly used this in the past, but once you become enlightened to the process, you will be using it at will. You will have customers agreeing with you all the way to the bank. When I first learned this, I used it everywhere and with everyone. It became a fun game for me to play with friends, family, customers, and complete strangers. After all, practice makes perfect and this is something you want to be perfect at.

If you end a statement with a question tone, then the person will automatically nod their head "yes" in agreement, even though there was no question being asked. For example, say to someone this next sentence with the voice intonation up, and watch them nod in agreeance, "This is the perfect house to raise a family in." Did you notice the person you were speaking to nod their head in agreeance?

The reason someone nods in agreeance is because the voice intonation that ended the sentence was with an upswing indicating a question was asked, and remember the brain is conditioned to answer questions. In fact, the brain is wired in such a way it feels a compelling need to answer questions. Try it and see for yourself. So, if you understand this and use it while speaking with people, you can have them agreeing with you repeatedly. The more the person agrees with you, the easier it will be for them to agree on the product, service, or numbers. Does this make sense to you?

Additionally, by using the command tone (intonation down), you can have the customer act when you want them to act. If you say, "Go ahead and sign here" with your voice intonation up, then the customer will be confused momentarily and could possibly give you a reason why they do not want to sign. However, if you say, "Go ahead and sign here" with a command tone, and it can be subtle, it doesn't have to be overbearing, the customer will feel the internally conditioned need to obey the command. Ahhhhh, the magic of words. Have you gotten that aha moment yet? If so, keep reading. If not, don't worry, keep reading you will get it soon.

You can ask a question with the intonation down, a command intonation, and have the same effect as saying a command sentence. For instance, "This is the home that you absolutely love and feel comfortable with, isn't it." Say it with the command intonation. It creates the feeling that you are telling them. Whereas, if you ask the same question, but this time with the question intonation, it will only sound like a question.

Often, when you ask a question, a person will not respond. Has that ever happened to you? The next time it happens, repeat the question, but only this time, use a command intonation and you will get the response you were looking for. When you use the command intonation at the end of your question, the customer, or whoever you are speaking with, will feel the internal need instilled since childhood to answer you. Voila, no more unanswered questions.

Practice using intonation often until you perfect it. Use it with the people you speak with on a daily basis and with your clients and notice the amazing results you get with it. You will be amazed at how something so simple can have such profound results. Make a game out of it like I did to make it even more exciting.

When you first learn how to play a game, it is exciting and challenging, isn't it? For instance, take the first time you learned how to play Monopoly. The first time you slowly pulled the blue board out of the box, opened it up, and set it on the table and become aware of all the real estate you can purchase; the railroads, the utility companies, the low end properties and of course the highline properties Board Walk and Park Place are jumping off of the board screaming, "Purchase Me! Purchase Me!" you felt the excitement from your feet all the way to the top of your head.

But, once you understand the rules and principles of the game, your confidence and excitement grew even more and the game became easier to play and your odds of winning increased, didn't it? You understand that by purchasing all of the similar color properties, that you can then begin to build little green homes on them and once you build four green homes, you can then construct a nice big red hotel which will bring in nice big bucks when another player lands on it. The same is true for sales.

It is an exciting industry where the sky is the limit on the income you are able to earn and once you understand the rules and principles of the sales process, you will grow more confident and more excited making it easy to play with your percentage of closing skyrocketing.

Practice over and over and over until you have mastered the skill of fact finding. Albert Einstein once said, "You have to learn the rules of the game. And then you have to play better than anyone else." Once you master the skill of fact finding, the door of success opens even wider for you.

CHAPTER 5

CREATING POWERFUL ELEVATOR PITCHES

"It's not about having the right opportunities. It's about handling the opportunities right."

Mark Hunter

The Elevator Pitch

The elevator pitch is simply powerful. If used properly, it will allow you to instantly capture someone's attention and have them begging to know more about whatever it is you do. Once you learn these powerful elevator pitches and use them naturally in a conversation, you will be amazed at the influx of new clients you will have.

Now, keep in mind, you do not need to know all of the pitches. Find the ones that you like the most and learn them so well that when you use them they will sound natural, not scripted. You do not want to sound like a robot. Sounding like a robot will not earn you the business you are looking for, instead, it is a sure fire way of looking like someone who is nervous and out of their element. You are a sales professional, so, sound like it.

First, before we get started, let's get something clear. An elevator pitch is not the same thing as a sales pitch. An elevator pitch is a different ball game all together. A sales pitch is a sales presentation. During a sales presentation, you typically have ample time to present the product or service you are attempting to sell with time allowed for objections to be brought up and overcome.

Elevator pitches, on the other hand, are used in social events, conferences, trade shows, when you meet someone while you are out running your errands, or waiting in line for a Starbucks coffee. The elevator pitch is used when time is of the essence and you only have a few seconds up to maybe two minutes to elicit someone's emotions and peak their interest enough to want to know more.

In a very short period of time, you want to get the other person interested in what you do, not bored with a lot of fluff. So make it powerful, interesting, and intriguing. Most people use the elevator pitch only to get a prospect's (and from this moment forward, we will be using the terms prospect, client, and customer interchangeably) card or to give them theirs. After learning these persuasive and powerful elevator pitches, you will not be a part of the majority who use it to get or give a business card, you will be using them to get the deal!

Typically, people are not good at things because they have not practiced them enough or are practicing the wrong technique and the elevator pitch is no different. If you are a sales professional, you want to make sure every area of your successful sales formula is practiced and topnotch. If it isn't, the only person you can get upset with about your commission check not being big enough is you. Every professional practices and perfects their craft. I advise you to do the same if you want to be in the top in your field and earn a lot of money

Here are a few ways salesmen sabotage their elevator pitches:

- Talk too much

- Use too much industry jargon

- Stand awkwardly and/or unconfidently

- Not enough eye contact

- It's too formal

- Too focused on who you are instead of benefit you offer

- Does not sound natural

So, to avoid these common mistakes that salesmen make and hinder their income, here are several proven elevator pitches you can implement in your repertoire to increase your bottom line.

With each of these examples below, I want you to grab your laptop or a notepad and something to write with, and begin writing 10 examples of your own that will work for you and your business. Remember, you will only be as good as your sales technique and process. The better technique and process you have, the better living you will earn.

Examples of Elevator Pitches:

Wow, How, Now

The **"*Wow, How, Now*" method** is simple, fun and grabs attention right away. It was created by Brian Walter, a communications consultant and founder of Extreme Meetings Inc. Brian explains that with the *Wow, How, Now method*, "you will create surprise and interest the second you open your mouth," and that by, "revealing what you do in an engaging *Wow, How, Now* sequence, you connect with a dialogue instead of a self-sabotaging monologue," which is very important. The last thing you want to do is bore someone to death or verbally assault them while you are trying to earn their business.

1. "*WOW*" You want to say something humorous, intriguing, or even puzzling that will make the other person want to hear more. It's a creative summary of what you do that demands some clarification.

2. "*HOW*" Answer the stated (or unspoken) question and explain exactly what you do.

3. "*NOW*" Shift into storytelling mode, giving solid examples of a current customer.

Examples:

Prospect: So, what do you do?

Me: I'm a success advisor.

Prospect: Huh?

Me: I am a coach who helps my clients find clarity in their business needs and assists in creating the most powerful and efficient path to achieve their desired goals and create a system of accountability.

For instance, my latest client was finally able to clear the roadblocks that were keeping her from finishing her book and now, she has gone on to land on the New York Times best seller list.

Prospect: So, what do you do?

Me: I help create money machines.

Prospect: Huh?

Me: I teach people how to use their language patterns more effectively in sales. Right now, I'm working with a consulting firm to train all their senior sales consultants on how to create unstoppable confidence and sales closes that will have prospects literally handing them their business.

Prospect: So, what do you do?

Me: I help people lie, steal, and drink.

Prospect: Huh?

Me: I assist people in locating their dream vacation home. Now, for instance, I'm working with a young couple who are looking to locate their dream beach home that will enable them to lie with the one they love, steal away beautiful days to always share together, and drink in the moments that will take their breath away.

Prospect: So, what do you do?

Me: I'm a sculptor.

Prospect: Huh?

Me: I have specifically designed programs for the couch potato that has never worked out a day in his or her life and wants to run a 5k, to the weekend warrior that is just looking to improve their level of fitness.

These scientifically designed programs have helped to sculpt my current client's body from one they were depressed living with into the body they truly desire, full of energy and strength, quickly and easily.

S.I.R. Framework

Another great elevator pitch is the S.I.R. Framework based on storytelling principles created by Gartner analyst, Richard Fouts. The principle is based upon creating conflict, escalating the conflict, and then resolving the conflict. This is one of the first pitches I learned in the car business.

1. Situation (conflict) - Create or illustrate the pain of a current situation.

2. Impact (escalate conflict) – Explain the impact of that situation.

3. Resolution – Explain how you solve the problem.

Examples:

Prospect: So, what do you do?

Me: Well, you know how most sales people try to execute a smooth and successful sales process, but do a poor job at it? Well, poor language patterns and a poor sales process have been proven to be the reason behind it.

When salesmen are ignorant to persuasive language patterns that get people to buy and are ignorant to a successful sales process that works; sales don't close, money is lost, not only for the salesman but also the company, as there are no referrals to take advantage of, and a lot of time gets wasted.

My company shows salespeople how to become top producers by implementing a proven successful sales process and using powerful hypnotic language patterns to capture those sales, bring in more referrals, and become more efficient with their time.

Prospect: So, what do you do?

Me: You know how most of the time when you go to buy a new car, it is a looooong (emphasize the word that you want to attach more emotion to) drawn out painful process where the car salesman is like a robot, going back and forth and back and forth from you to the sales manager to see if he can get you a better deal and when you finally do buy after spending allllll day at the dealership, you are not even sure if you got a good deal or not, you were just ready to leave?

Well, I can change all of that for you. If you, like me, like to enjoy your day, and time is valuable to you, then you will absolutely look forward to buying your next car from me.

Straight to the Point

Here is a straight to the point elevator pitch from Benay of Universal Coaching Systems, for the no nonsense prospect. Remember, you need to quickly gauge your prospect and know which powerful weapon to use in order to earn their business, or at the very least, earn the opportunity to present your sales pitch for a later date.

Hi, I'm *"name"* from company *"name"*.

I am a *"description"* for *"client's type"*.

"Give a cool statistic related to your specific business or to your niche as a whole." One thing that makes my business stand out from my competitors is *"blank"*.

Something I am looking for right now is *"blank"*.

If you have any ideas, I'd love to discuss them with you after the meeting.

Examples:

Hi, I'm Benay from Universal Coaching Systems.

I am a product development expert who works specifically with coaches.

I've already helped almost 2,000 coaches from all over the world create their first coaching products!

One thing that makes my business stand out from my competitors' is that I personally do what I love, feel totally fulfilled by my choices, and lead a balanced and free life on my terms. My business teaches others how to do the same from a place of trust and integrity.

Something I am looking for right now is new and creative ways to get even more coaches using our Life Coach Office coaching software.

If you have any ideas, I'd love to discuss them with you after the meeting.

Hi, I'm Mike Smith with 123 Realty.

I am a top producing real estate expert who works specifically with commercial real estate investors.

My firm has closed more contracts this month than most other firms close all year. What this means for our clients is they are guaranteed to be working with a company who knows how to get the best deals, best opportunities, and get the transaction completed quickly and efficiently.

One thing that makes my firm stand out from my competitors is that ninety percent of our business is repeat and referral business. That means a lot to us here at 123 Realty.

Something I am looking for right now is earning new business which will allow others to experience the same investment and return opportunities that our current clients are happily experiencing.

If you or someone you know would be interested in making sound investments, I'd love to speak with them about it.

Hi, I'm Daniel Austin with 123 Motors.

I am the top salesman who works specifically with customers looking to get the best deal on a car.

Our dealership is involved in more charities and community functions than all the other dealerships in town combined, and coincidentally, we sell more cars than those other dealerships combined too.

One thing that makes our dealership stand out from the competition is that we are very transparent with the entire sales process. Our cars have no "haggle" pricing. And you see the options from the lenders and their interest rates the same time we do so you get to choose the one you feel most comfortable with. This way, you do not have to worry if you received the best deal when you leave our dealership, you already know you did.

If you or someone you know is looking to get a great deal on a new or pre-owned vehicle, I'd love to speak with them.

Let Me Ask You A Question

This is similar to the *Wow, How, Now* method, but with a little extra. It asks a question, which gets the prospect involved enough to engage fully in the conversation taking place and it also has a "call to action" tag question. One of the most powerful elevator pitches I have seen or used.

Examples:

Prospect: So, What do you do?

Me: I'm a marketing engineer.

Prospect: Huh?

Me: Let me ask you a question. (If you know the person is a self-help author) Do you currently have a strategy in place to enable you to reach your sales goals? No. Well, I help authors just like you who are launching a new book they want to be successful, reach their sales goals, and help others in the process.

Where I help my clients is in the powerful, proven formula my company provides in the key areas of marketing and advertising. As a result, they're able to quickly and easily achieve the recognition and profitability they desire. Is this something you're interested in? Great! Let's get started.

Prospect: So, what do you do?

Me: I'm an investment engineer.

Prospect: Huh?

Me: Let me ask you a question. What if you there was a way you could invest a fraction of your money that would allow you to retire in 15 years, would you be interested to find out how?

Prospect: So, what do you do?

Me: I'm a persuasion engineer specialist.

Prospect: Huh?

Me: Suppose there was a way you could quickly train your sales team to easily and naturally implement a persuasive and hypnotic sales language that is proven to close more sales, would you be interested in finding out how?

Prospect: So, what do you do?

Me: I'm dream manufacturer.

Prospect: Huh?

Me: Let me ask you a question. Suppose your dream was to be in the best shape of your life, starting your own business, or finding the ideal mate, and I told you that I know a scientifically proven formula for you to achieve your dream, would you be interested in finding out how?

I Make People Forget Things

The "I make people forget things" method is one that peaks the interest and imagination instantly. It is simple, straight to the point, and will almost always make the other person say, "Huh?"

Examples:

Prospect: So, what do you do?

Me: I make people forget things.

Prospect: Huh?

Me: It's quite simple really. Most people want to be successful in their career, but aren't exactly sure how, don't you agree? Albert Einstein once said, "Continuing to do the same thing over and over again is insanity."

I help people to forget about doing the things that do not work in achieving their desired result and excitedly get them to start implementing a proven process that does work. When would be a good time this week to show you how easy it can be?

Prospect: So, what do you do?

Me: I make people forget things.

Prospect: Huh?

Me: It's quite simple really. Most people want to drop a few pounds and get into shape, but get overwhelmed by all of the choices of exercises to do such as cardio, aerobic, anaerobic, calisthenics, weight training, etc. and overwhelmed by what they should and should not eat, don't you agree?

I make people forget about all of those choices and get them out of overwhelm, making things simple and fun by beginning with one of my specifically designed and scientifically proven exercise and nutrition programs, which is easy to follow and guaranteed to help drop the weight and get into shape.

Prospect: So, what do you do?

Me: I make people forget things.

Prospect: Huh?

Me: It's quite simple really. Most people have bought a car before and have had a bad experience, don't you agree? Well, I help people forget all about that negative car buying experience by giving them the best customer service, best price, and best experience they have ever had.

Prospect: So, what do you do?

Me: I make people forget things.

Prospect: Huh?

Me: It's quite simple really. Most businesses want to run as efficiently as possible and to increase their profit margins, but due to managers being improperly trained and unaware of the areas in which they need attention, increasing profit margins and running efficiently is a daunting task, don't you agree?

Well, my firm helps hard working business owners just like yourself, forget about the lack of proper training his managers received and the profits not being where they would like, by fast tracking his managers on a proven Management Success Course specifically designed to create efficiency in the workplace and increase profit margins.

What's It Like When You

This one is great because it automatically has the prospect activating their imagination and feeling or seeing what you want (outcome) them to and lets the prospect know that you <u>can </u>provide the outcome.

Examples:

What's it like when you persuade someone to make the right decision? Very satisfying, isn't it? Well, my company helps car salesmen to close more deals and get more referrals with ease, instantly, by using persuasive language patterns that are used by the CIA, the Secret Service, and the top sales professionals around the world to get what they want. Is morning or afternoon a better time to meet and discuss this in further detail?

What's it like when you purchase something that you absolutely love and know that it was a great decision? Well, hold that feeling because that's what I do. I help my clients' purchase the right home they will absolutely love and know will be a great decision. That is what you want, isn't it? What time this week is good for you to sit down and share with me your wants, needs and desires for your new home?

(A slight variation) What would it be like when your life is in perfect balance and you feel completely happy inside and out? It would be very satisfying, would it not? Well, that is what I do. I'm a life coach who focuses on personal development to create balance and an overwhelming sense of happiness inside and out. When would you like to begin to be completely happy?

What's it like when you feel completely at peace because you know the financial future of your loved ones is taken care of? Very satisfying isn't it? That's what I do. I help loving husbands and fathers just like you select the right life insurance policy that will make sure their loved ones are completely taken care of when they pass on. Would Wednesday or Friday be better for you to spend some time with me and discuss the right policy for your loving family?

You should have noticed by now, that some of these elevator pitches have questions at the end that ask for the sale. Now, the elevator pitch is for you to grab the prospect's attention and then grab the business. So once the prospect seems interested, ask for the business or an opportunity to meet with them. Ask questions such as:

- Since you're interested, when is the best time to meet with you for more details? Would this week or next week be better for you?

- I have some time available later in the week. What time do you have available to discuss this further?

- Since you're interested and we are both busy right now, let's go ahead and schedule a time where we can discuss this in further detail.

- Tomorrow is good for me to sit and discuss this further, how about you?

The elevator pitch is a powerful tool to use that will allow you to capture someone's attention and have them begging to know what you do. Once they are interested in what you do, ask for the business.

When this technique is used properly, you will surely see an influx of clients and money. Go ahead and imagine now, the multitude of prospects you will have instantly turned into happy clients and customers. Imagine how your finances will change by naturally and effortlessly using these proven elevator pitches. Looks and feels good doesn't it?

CHAPTER 6

TOP SALES CLOSES

"You miss 100% of the sales you do not ask for"

The Close

The close is the most important part of the entire sales
process because without this crucial step, nothing
happens. You could have executed the sales process
flawlessly by asking all the right questions, eliciting all
the right emotions, having everyone in agreeance, even
have the prospect fall in love with what you have but if
you do not ask for the sale your customer does not get
to enjoy your product and you make absolutely no
money. You both walk away empty handed. And thanks

to you not asking the most important question everyone's time was wasted.

You see, you miss 100% of the sales you do not ask for. You must ask for the sale. Think about it, what is the worst that could happen? Someone tell you "no" and walk off and you never see them again? If this does happen then what have you really lost? Nothing. You can't lose something you didn't have to begin with. Ask for the sale. I have seen so many salespeople go through the entire process and not ask for the sale because they did not want to seem pushy. It is like purchasing a raffle ticket at an auction and not checking to see if you won the grand prize. If you do not check to see if you have the winning ticket then the prize will go to someone else. And another salesperson will easily close the deal, because you have already done the hard part. A lot of sales are simply made because they were asked for. There are a lot of people out there that already do all of the necessary research on the product and are ready to buy all they need is someone to ask them.

I was selling Olhausen pool tables for a while and I had this young gentleman on the show floor looking at this beautiful 8 foot contemporary pool table with black felt for $6,000. You could tell he liked it. He was touching the top rails and admiring the color. While he was leaning back slightly rubbing his chin I simply walked over to him and said, "Looks good doesn't it?" He replied, "Yes it does." With a smile on his face. So, I said, "You should go ahead and buy it." Which he responded with, "Alright, let's do it." Now, not all sales will be that simple and easy but you will have some that are. You just have to ask.

And if salespeople miss a sale, we play the "What if" game don't we? "What if I would have said this instead?" "What if I would have done this instead?" "What if I could have closed two more deals this week?" "What if I was a better salesperson than I am?" "What if I made more money?" But the fact that you are reading this book means that you are ready to close every deal you possibly can. You are not going to let anyone get past you. You are tired of playing the "What if" game and because you are reading this book, you are easily absorbing all of the powerful information inside and you will be able to effortlessly use the patterns and techniques inside this book on everyone you speak to. Now, the only questions are how many people do you want to talk to in a day and how much business do you want?

Most sales people spend too much time talking, and the things they say just don't work. Learn how to say just the right amount and get the results you are looking for. Because if you talk too much, and seasoned salespeople can back me up on this, you can talk yourself right out of the sale. Knowing what to say and how much to say will make you a closing machine. I am about to expose you to the top proven sales closes from the top closers in the world. These closes have earned sale after high grossing sale, easily and effortlessly. Learning these sales will turn you into a top grossing, industry leading selling machine and the thing you will like the most is that while everyone else thinks you are busting your ass putting in grueling 60 hour work weeks to achieve the results you do, you will sit back and secretly know that you are doing this with ease. In fact, you will be doing this with less time and effort than almost everyone else because of your absolute confidence in your entire sales process and the precision of your persuasive hypnotic language patterns, you will have everyone asking, "How do you do it?"

Have you ever bought something and while you were paying for the product, you said to yourself, "How did this happen? I didn't plan on buying anything." I sold a car to a gentleman once and when he was getting ready to leave, smiling ear to ear, he told me, "Danny, I did not plan on buying a car today. I was just here with a friend that was buying his car." This gentleman loved his new Chevy Camaro and the experience so much that he sent me several referrals and a thank you card. I've had numerous customers tell me that they were, "Just beginning to look at cars and we are not going to buy today" but ended up buying from me that day. They would tell me smiling and laughing, "Danny, how did you do this? I did not plan on buying a car today but you just made this so easy. Thanks."

I have also had it happen to me and I am well versed in the techniques. I remember standing at the register, pulling out my credit card and thinking to myself, "What am I doing? I don't even need this new coat." Then I smiled and said to myself, "That guy was good." No matter how versed you are, if the techniques are executed properly, you will be helpless. I am going to go through a few examples of the most powerful closes that will leave your prospects with only one answer to give you, "YES." The word yes is a great word, isn't it? Think about it for a moment, the first time your significant other said "yes" to your invitation for a date, or the first "yes" you heard while pitching a product, or the first "yes" you received when requesting a raise. Yes feels very good right now, doesn't it?

But, before we go over these powerful closes I want to talk to you about the two reasons people want to purchase a product or service. Once you know and understand these two reasons you will then have a better understanding of when to use the closes and be able to tailor fit them to your customers and their needs. Remember earlier in the first chapter of this book I talked about the two factors that directly influence motivation? That people either move away from problems or towards goals. Well the same two factors that influence motivation are the same two factors that will influence your customer to purchase your product.

Towards Or Away From Selling

Every one of your customers will fall into one of these two categories. They will either be in category A. Those that move towards achieving or accomplishing a goal or category B. Those moving away from the pain of not achieving or accomplishing the goal. They both have the same end result in mind, goal attainment, but have two totally different perceptions of what the goal means to them and why they should attain it.

Take for instance, if you sell cars, and have a customer who just walked into the dealership and you greet them and during the discovery phase of the sales process you ask, "So Mr. Ross, what is important to you with your next vehicle? Are there any specific features you would like or have to have?" Let them respond. Then the next question you ask is where you will discover if they are motivated by towards or away from values. So pay close attention to their answer. The next question you will ask is, "Why is that important to you?" Or, "Why is (X) important to you?" The reason this is so important and powerful is that it will allow you to determine if they are moving towards a goal or away from a pain, and also allow you to set up your sales pitch and close the deal.

If your customer responds with something to the effect of, "I want a good reliable car that is good on gas and it has to have navigation." You could follow up with, "Mr. Ross I understand how you feel. Our customers felt the same way and what they found was that the selection of vehicles we offer here at XYZ Motors provides them with exactly that, a good reliable car, and they now refer us to their family and friends. Now, tell me, why is navigation important to you?" Then listen to their response carefully. If they respond with, "Because it will allow me to get to my destination quickly and easily." Or, "It will help me save time driving to my appointments."

These answers are towards values answers. They are motivated to achieve and accomplish. So the influencing words you want to use in your sales pitch with these type of customers would be words such as; benefit, advantage, accomplish, achieve, obtain, to get, and other words that are about achieving. Now you can respond with, "I can definitely understand that Mr. Ross. The great thing about the cars we have on our lot is that they either have navigation that will allow you to save time driving to your appointments or we can install it.

If the customer responds with, "I am tired of getting lost." Or, "It will help me not waste time driving to my appointments." These answers are away from values answers. They are motivated to move away from pain. So the influencing words you want to use in your sales pitch with these type of customers would be; prevent, avoid, fix, won't have to, there will be not problems. Now you can respond with, "I can definitely understand that Mr. Ross. The great thing about the cars we have on our lot is that they either have navigation so you will not get lost, or we can have it installed for you."

By responding in this subtle but particular way the customer feels that you are really listening to them and understand their wants and needs. It is very important to listen to what your customers are saying. The quicker you learn this invaluable little secret the quicker you will begin to easily and effortlessly close more deals. Know and understand what your customers want to accomplish. Are they trying to achieve a goal or avoid a pain? If they are trying to achieve a goal then show them how they can achieve it with your product. If they are trying to avoid a pain then show them how they can avoid it with your product. Learning this simple sales technique will significantly boost your sales and increase your closing percentage.

Now, are you ready to learn the top proven sales techniques and principles for creating an unstoppable sales close that will enable you to sell anything? Good. Let's get started.

"Sales are contingent upon the attitude of the salesman – not the attitude of the prospect."

W. Clement Stone

<u>Closing Techniques</u>

The imagination is one of the most powerful tools you can use to sell your product. Get your prospect to envision themselves owning or using your product or service and you are half way home to the sell. Albert Einstein said, "Imagination is the preview of life's coming attractions." Get your customer to take mental ownership of what you are selling them. Get their emotions involved. The more your customer mentally owns your product the easier it will be for them to financially own it. As you may already know, getting them to take mental ownership is a giant leap in the right direction of closing the sale.

After you finish reading each section, take out a notepad or your laptop and something to write with, and begin creating your own power closes using the structure you just learned. Come up with at least ten closes per section pertaining to whatever field you are in. You should do this because the more you practice these hypnotic language patterns, the more ingrained the language patterns will become. The easier they become, the easier it will be for you to speak them without even thinking about them and the easier it will be for you to make a lot more money.

1. Just suppose... These two words unlock your prospect's mind and will allow them to imagine anything you want them to. These two words will also allow your prospect to create the image of your outcome with far less critical judgement, which is what you want.

- Just suppose you were to take this training course. How can you see it changing your life?

- Just suppose you learned covert, hypnotic language patterns and applied them to every one of your prospects. How would your finances change?

- Just suppose all of your objections were to melt away and you decided to make a down payment today, knowing that you'll find a way to cover the payments. When would you want to take delivery, now?

- Just suppose you took delivery today, who would be more excited, you or your spouse?

- I know you don't have the money right now, but just suppose you were able to come up with it, where are some of the places or who could you borrow the investment from?

- Just suppose you purchased this insurance policy, and there was an incident that required you to file an insurance claim and we saved you a lot of time and thousands of dollars. How would you feel then?

- I know you don't think you have the need for this policy right now, but just suppose you had an unforeseen incident happen and this policy enabled you to replace what was lost and have

- extra money to do what you want. How would you feel then?

- Just suppose you purchased this home, how would you decorate it?

2. Don't (action) unless you want (your outcome).

This is one of the most covert patterns I have learned because the action and the outcome do not even have to be related, as long as the relationship sounds reasonable.

You see, when you use the cause and effect pattern, the prospects have to imagine themselves doing the action, and they will be bound to follow through with the outcome. The human mind is a very intricate machine, yet still very simple. It searches for reasons why things happen so there is a sense of certainty.

If a person is told that one thing happens as a direct result of something else, they will relate the two as being true. This caused that and because of that, the action can be either positive or negative. Are you ready to have some fun with this one?

- Don't even think about driving this car home unless you want to make everyone in the neighborhood jealous.

- Don't even consider taking this training unless you are ready to make more money than you ever have before.

- Do not test drive this car unless you are ready to fall in love with its luxury and performance.

- Don't even put an offer on this home unless you are ready to live in the home of your dreams.

- Don't sign this contract unless you are absolutely sure your company is ready to increase productivity and revenue.

- Don't even consider buying this car now unless you are ready to enjoy the gas savings and riding with the top down and the sun on your face.

• Don't even think about hiring me unless you are absolutely sure you want the results we discussed earlier from your team.

• Don't even consider going with our company unless you are ready to make changes and become number one in your industry.

3. What would happen if (your outcome), and/because (their value). This is another powerful pattern, which will anchor their value to your outcome. You will find this very similar to the, cause equals effect pattern. Keep in mind to only use the values that the client gives you, not one you assume for your client.

• What would happen if you purchased our training and you increased your company's efficiency and revenue?

• What would happen if you invested in this property and the property's value doubled?

- What would happen if you invested in your firm because you want to save money?

- What would happen if you purchased this truck because you wanted to pull your boat to the lake every weekend?

- What would happen if you used our consulting firm because we are known for getting results and you received the results you are looking for?

- What would happen if you invested in yourself because you truly believe the benefits outweigh the investment?

- What would happen if your company hired our team to reorganize and restructure your management team and the team worked better than ever before, with fewer mistakes, and your company's moral grew to the highest level it has ever been?

- What would happen if you drove this car home today because it was the car of your dreams, and your spouse fell in love with it too?

4. Wouldn't you like/love to (your outcome)? This hypnotic pattern is great because it gets the client to imagine the product or service and gets their emotions involved at the same time. You see, for the client to know if they will love the product or service, they have to first imagine themselves using the product or service, and loving the product or service.

- Wouldn't you love to be in the best shape of your life and have the same energy and vitality you had as a twenty year old?

- Wouldn't you like your kids to grow up in a safe area with a great school system so they can get the best education possible?

- Wouldn't you love to finally treat yourself after all these years of hard work and get the car you have always dreamed of? You have always done for others, don't you think they would be happy you finally did something for yourself now?

- Wouldn't you like to have your company become aware of the areas they could improve efficiency, which will increase your revenue and build a strong sense of unity within the staff?
- Wouldn't you love to see your wife smile the biggest smile you have ever seen after she opens this box of beautiful diamond earrings you specifically chose for her?

- Wouldn't you love to walk into your bedroom and feel as if you are in a luxurious five star resort? Imagine walking through your beautifully decorated room to lie on the most comfortable bed you have ever laid on after a long stressful day of work. Feels good, doesn't it?

- Wouldn't you like to hire a team that has your best interest at heart and a reputation that gets results?

- Wouldn't you like to be so persuasive with your closing techniques that you are the top producer in the company?

5. Can you imagine (your outcome)? And then you can give them their primary motives for buying with a tag question. Again, another good close due to the fact that it gets emotions and justify with logic is to sell to people's emotion and anchor great emotional states to whatever it is you are selling. This will guarantee you a deal.

- Can you imagine how happy your kids will be growing up in a house like this? They will each have their own room and a huge backyard to play in. They will like that, won't they?

- Can you imagine what you would do with all of the money you will get on an investment like this? This investment is safe, long-term, and will yield you the money you are looking for, won't it?

- Can you imagine how excited your spouse will be about the purchase of this timeshare? You said your spouse loved traveling to different beaches for vacations and likes to save money while doing it. This is the perfect gift for her, isn't it?

- Can you imagine all the excess weight you will drop and the confidence you will gain by fitting in the clothes you want to by using our product?
- Can you imagine using these hypnotic and persuasive language patterns effortlessly and easily closing your clients?

6. Have you found (your outcome) makes/gives you (benefit)? This pattern has the powerful, "Oh, not yet," close built into it if you need it. This pattern allows you to have your prospect construct the mental image of your outcome. It is an assumptive close that allows you to say, "Oh, not yet" to the question you are looking for a yes to.

• Have you found that using the sample of our product over just this short period gives you the energy you are looking for and a healthier glow to your skin?

• Have you found that by using a company like ours, you can have your internet business making you more money than ever before? "No." Oh, not yet? Here, let me show you...

• Have you found that making the right decision and getting the right equipment for the job the first time saves you money and time? "No." Oh, not yet? Our customers have saved thousands of dollars and countless of hours by going with the Gulfstream G-IVSP because...

• Have you found that when you purchase the right type of jewelry, it not only looks sumptuous, but becomes a family heirloom?

- Have you found that when you invest in yourself, it is something that you can always get excited about and feel the confidence build because you know you deserve it?

7. Hypnotic Instant Replay With Tag Questions.
Repeat client's wants/needs/values and place a tag question at the end. This one is extremely powerful because you can use it in various ways. It shows the client that you are listening with their best interest at heart and gets them to agree, which is another yes, and helps to overcome objections before they begin.

Make sure to repeat the client's own words back to them, not your own words of what was said. Example, if the client says, "I want a policy that takes the weight off of my shoulders. I finally have my dream home on the lake, the perfect boat, and the Platinum Edition Escalade. Everything is going perfect in my life and I want to make sure the family is taken care of when I die, but I do not want to pay more than $400 a month." Do not respond with, "Mr. Jones, I will get you the perfect policy that will give you ample coverage for all of your needs.

- "Correct me if I'm wrong Mr. Jones, but you want a policy that takes the weight off of your shoulders, because you finally have your dream home on the lake, the perfect boat, and the Platinum Edition Escalade, and you said you want a policy that will take care of the family when you die, but you do not want to pay more than $400 a month. If I have a policy like this, you are ready to sign today, right?"

- "Mrs. Han, you said this was the perfect home because it was right on the beach, within walking distance of shopping and dining, and came in under your budget, didn't you?"

- "Mr. Ayers, you told me that learning these hypnotic language patterns and teaching them to your salesmen will enable you to easily increase your store's revenue, right? Will you be attending the workshop alone or will you be bringing someone with you?"

- "Mr. Schell, you said you wanted to work with a company that thoroughly trained their staff, had room for advancement, benefits, a starting salary between $70,000 and $75,000, and also had a short commute because of the gas prices, right? Our company meets those requirements. When would you like to start, this Monday or the following Monday?"

- "So, Mr. McGinnis, what you are saying is if I was able to get you the fleet of work vans you are looking at here for only $18,000 each, and had them delivered to your company by the 15th, then you are ready to make the deal today?"

- "Correct me if I'm wrong Mr. Thomas, I just want to make sure I understand everything correctly. You said if can get you $8,000 for completing the home restoration on these two homes, that you will be finished with the project no later than ten days, correct?"

Let a person completely change their thought process of the sale and implement techniques and principles that are proven to work and they will be astonished at the how quickly the transformation will take place in their finances. The most dominant athletes in the world dominate because they continually study, practice, and hone their skills. They continually execute the proven process with the proven techniques and proven principles. They know that if they do not, they will be replaced by someone else who is practicing more and wants to be at the top more than they do. Kobe Bryant knew this even back in high school. In high school when most kids sleep in and complain about having to get up for school Kobe was up at 5 a.m. every morning practicing. He knew that if he wanted to be better than everyone else he had to put in more work than everybody else. He carried this intense and determined work ethic over into the NBA, as well, and worked harder than any basketball player that ever graced the court, even Michael Jordan, according to Phil Jackson in one of his interviews.

His sheer determination to win and practice harder than everyone else is what made it so easy for him to dominate during actual games and has made him one of the greatest basketball players ever to play the game. The top sales professionals in all sales fields across the globe are enlightened with this same truth, "When you are not honing your skills, someone else is, someone who wants to take your place." That is the reason they continue to hone their skills with continual practice and role play. To be the best, you have to be prepared to be the best.

Just as top athletes and top sales professionals in the world are enlightened with this knowledge, so now are you. You will now grow to understand how to become a far more effective and efficient sales professional. Closing with confidence and ease, and filled with more passion for life than you may even have thought possible once you allow yourself to model and reproduce the same techniques and results from those who have already achieved excellence.

Have you noticed that the most sought after motivational speakers speak the same message at each event? Grant Cardone, Anthony Robbins, Les Brown, and everyone else all speak their own unique but same message. Now, don't get me wrong, they have several speeches in their arsenal, but they tell their same speech over and over again. Why? Because it works! Out of experience they know that particular speech is the absolute best speech to get the desired results from their audience. That's why.

Now, imagine how using these powerful, time tested proven techniques can change your career. Imagine the amount of deals you will be closing, imagine your bank account growing bigger and bigger and bigger and imagine everyone asking you to teach them to do what you do.

Just for a moment, I want you to take a deep breath and just relax and imagine now, if you can, easily and effortlessly using the closes you just learned. How can your life change? How could it be better? What most excites you about learning what you just learned? You see, excitement is a great thing, it is an extremely powerful emotion that can keep you motivated to continue doing what you want and do it better than everyone else.

The more excitement about your profession you have the better you will be and the quicker you will become number one. The more you practice the more your excitement will increase because you will be excited to execute your skills and close more deals. Your excitement will continue to grow more and more which will cause your enjoyment for your profession to also grow more and more, until you are the top salesperson at your company and you are teaching others what techniques and principles you used to get you there. Doesn't that make you excited?

CHAPTER 7

OVERCOMING OBJECTIONS

"Objections can reveal the missing piece of the puzzle that can put the deal together for you"

The words you use to overcome the objections your customers has are important, but the pattern in which you use them in is crucial / more important. If you use the right patterns you will persuade your customers to move forward with the purchase of your product or service. If you do not use the right patterns then you will struggle with every customer you have. This is why it is imperative that you, like other successful salespeople, learn powerful proven patterns to easily overcome objections. The better you get at overcoming objections the easier selling will become for you. The easier selling becomes for you the more money you will make.

What Are Objections

Objections have stumbled and stopped every salesperson on the face of this Earth from making a sale somewhere along the way in their career. Especially in the beginning. At least, I know they did for me. I am pretty witty and can think on my feet but there was a time in the beginning of my sales career that I was scared of objections and froze like a deer in headlights when I encountered them. I used to think that since I was an honest, likeable person and since I was selling a good quality product that everyone should just "sign on up" with "no questions asked". So when they didn't "sign on up" with "no questions asked" and threw out an objection or two at me I didn't know what to do. It was like I was sitting in the batter's box waiting for a fastball down the middle but instead received a knuckleball. If you have ever been in the sales field I'm sure you can relate. And anyone in sales knows that not learning how to overcome objections will cost you money, a lot of money, and quite possibly your job.

So, I quickly learned, and so will you, that encountering objections just comes with the territory and shouldn't be anything to worry about. I discovered from years in the sales field, countless seminars, and extensive research that objections come in one of 3 types.

Three Types Of Objections

1. Objections are simply complaints. Studies show that a customer is much more likely to purchase your product or service after he/she has aired their complaint. Complaints you can simply acknowledge and move on.

2. Objections are a way for the customer to find out more information on an area that is important to them, before they purchase. In these instances you educate the customer on what it is they want to know.

3. Objections are sometimes a real objection. When they are a real objection you do what all top successful salespeople do. You use the proven techniques, you are about to discover, to overcome them with ease. The more times you read this book and use the powerfully persuasive techniques provided inside the easier you will overcome objections and grow your bank account.

There are 2 ways in handling objections:

1. Inoculate them before they occur

2. Develop persuasive scripts that handle objections smoothly

First we will talk about inoculating objections before they occur. This is by far the best way to handle objections. Because if you stop them before they occur then you will easily write up countless deals. But, if you are unable to stop them before they occur, no worries. You will learn the same powerful scripts used by top salespeople around the world to easily overcome them.

Absolutely Destroying Objections

Do you know how to absolutely destroy an objection? The best time to absolutely destroy objections is before they are even brought up, you inoculate them, also known as the "stop it before it starts" technique. You see, if you overcome the objection during the sales process, then at the close of the sale, there is nothing that can be brought up to sabotage it. Top sales professionals will take the premeasured steps before the close to stomp out any objection the customer would have had. How do you do this? I'm glad you asked. There are three steps to this simple technique.

Step One

Compile a list of all the objections you get from your clients or customers. You can do this alone or with the other salesmen you work with. If you do this with other salesmen, write down the objections they encounter also, as this will ensure that you will always be prepared for whatever might come your way. Write them all down and look at them.

There should only be a handful of objections because if there are a countless number of objections you repeatedly get, then you are not doing something right and hopefully after reading this book, you will know where you were going astray and find your way back. After getting all of the objections together, you move to step two.

Step Two

Structuring sentences to overcome the objections so they can't be brought up. For instance, if an objection you get is, "It is too expensive," then you should have a sentence that will destroy it during your presentation or somewhere along the way.

Ex. If you are selling jewelry and get the "it's not in my budget" objection often, you could possibly say in your pitch,

"This is a sumptuous diamond ring that your dear wife will love forever. Just imagine her excitedly showing it off to all of her friends and telling them how great of a husband you are and how much you love her. A happy wife is priceless, but can you believe I have some husbands come in here and tell me that the ring their wife deserves is too expensive? I mean, wow, you have to really not care about your wife to say something like that."

Ex. If you are selling life insurance and you get the policy is too expensive objection often, you could say in your pitch:

Mr. Customer, I don't want to sound rude but, I have a few customers that when we get to this point want to think about it before they make the decision to go ahead and buy life insurance. And the reason is usually they want to make sure they are making the right decision. Now, you do you feel this is the coverage you need, correct? And, you can afford it, correct? And, you feel comfortable with me being your very own personal life insurance agent, correct? Good.

Then, move on to the last and shortest step of the three-step process.

Step Three

Ask the customer if they have any more questions while you get the paperwork ready.

Review Of Steps To Absolutely Destroy Objections

1. Write down all of the objections you get from your customers.

2. Create sentences or phrases that destroy what their objections would be.

3. Ask for the sale.

"Customers will not buy until they know you care why they are buying"

There is also another technique to "stop it before it starts". It is by simply bringing up the objections before your customer does. Or the "I know what you're thinking" technique. What I mean is that if you believe your customer may bring up an objection such as; "need time to think about it" or "need to talk it over with my spouse" or "it's out of my budget" or any of the other common objections, then you bring it up first. It is similar to the first technique but instead of having it in the pitch itself you ask the question directly. What it does is put you in the driver's seat. You are in control and the objection can be dealt with effectively before it even becomes a real objection. This puts you in the position of a caring salesperson. Which you are. The customer sees you as being in tune with them and feels more comfortable with you and because of this, will give you their business.

With the next examples I want you to write down ways you can implement them into your sales situations and particular field. Write down as many as you can think of and make them perfect. They may not start out perfect and that is okay. What you want to do is continue to edit them until they are perfect. You want powerfully persuasive scripts that you will use with perfection every single time.

A few ways to implement the "I know what you're thinking" technique:

After spending a little time with you I would be willing to take a guess that you may be concerned with/about (X).

Mr. Customer, after spending a little time with you I would be willing to take a guess that you may be concerned about financing. One of the great things about our company is that we only use the top lenders in the industry and I can assure you that we will get you the best rate possible. The process is fast and easy. I recommend we do it now.

If I were in your position I would probably be thinking (X).

Mr. Customer If I were in your position I would probably be thinking, can this fitness book camp really get me into shape for my wedding? The short answer is, yes. Sign here and let's get started now because the sooner we get started the sooner you will be at your ideal weight and feel great for your wedding.

I bet you're asking yourself (X)?

Mr. Customer, I bet you're asking yourself, can I afford this sales training? And the question isn't, can you afford it, it's can you afford not to take it. After the sales training I guarantee that you will close more deals and make more money. And that is what you want right? Sign here to become a money making machine.

If you are concerned about (X).

Mr. Customer if you are concerned about the cost of the software don't worry, that is normal, you are not alone. Several of our clients were worried about the cost in the beginning but soon realized the money, time, and stress they were saving and could not thank us enough and wish they would have upgraded with us sooner. Sign here and begin saving money, time, and stress now.

You may be wondering (X).

Mr. Customer you may be wondering if we will be able to complete the project in time. And with the time constraints we are under it is a valid concern and I can assure you that we have completed projects the same size and complexity in shorter time frames with perfection. Sign here.

If you didn't close the deal and have your customer happily walk away you still have no need to worry because you can still easily overcome the objection you didn't know was there and close the deal with this next technique. An easy way to set the customer at ease and retrieve the vital information you need to close the sale is the:

"Before you leave" technique.

You simply ask the customer,

"Mr. and Mrs. Customer, I apologize. Did I do something wrong?"

The customer will usually respond with "No, why do you ask?"

Then you will respond with, "Well, I was under the impression that you felt this (insert product or service) was what you were looking for? Before you leave, do you mind sharing with me what concerns you had? Or is there anything that troubled you that might have stopped you from buying?"

Then, with the vital information the customer now gives you, which is exactly what they need to know before they purchase your product or service, you say,

"Oh, wow. I apologize." and give them the information they are looking for.

For instance, when I was young in my sales career selling cars, I had a sweet older couple who loved everything about the Chevy Suburban I was showing them. The wife selected the shiny black one with all the bells and whistles. She loved it, but I think her husband loved it more than she did. I thought to myself, this is a laydown (In the sales industry, for you who do not know, a laydown is someone who does not haggle or show any resistance to the sale) and was already thinking I would get two or three vehicles out that day because it was still early.

However, we were nearing the end of the process and they said, "Thank you for your time Mr. Cole, but we really need to be going as we have some errands to run. We will call you." At first, I didn't know what to do or think. I was in shock. Only a few moments earlier, the couple was excitedly conversing over where they were going to take the first vacation in the new Suburban. You see, they loved road trips and confirmed that it would fit in their three-car garage easily. So, keeping my composure and not letting them know I was shaken from the previous statement, I followed up with something powerful I learned from one of the other top salesmen at the dealership. The "before you leave" technique.

"Mr. and Mrs. McGinnis, I apologize. Did I do something wrong?" "No. Not at all, why do you ask" was the response I received. "I was under the impression that you felt this Suburban was the one you wanted. Before you leave, do you mind sharing with me what concerns you had? Or is there anything that troubled you that might have stopped you from buying?" I replied. Then, because their guard was down, they told me that they loved the vehicle, but they really wanted it in the white not black, and we didn't have white one on the lot. Then I said, "Oh, wow. I apologize again. I can have the white Suburban, the one you love and feel is right for you, delivered to your house, all I have to do is transfer one over from our other dealership. (Voice intonation up so they agree.) Now, all we need to do is easily finish up with this order and it's all yours. (Again, voice intonation up so they agree.)

Agreement Frame

Another amazingly persuasive technique to overcome objections is the Agreement Frame. The Agreement Frame is one of my favorite techniques because it bypasses resistance that a customer may have towards whatever the objection is and move in the direction of the sell. You see, if you disagree with someone, no matter what the topic is about, you invite a debate but, if you agree, then you move on. That is why I absolutely love the agreement frame. Now, it is crucial when using the Agreement Frame to use the word "and" instead of the word "but". The word "but" invites a debate and we do not want a debate. We want a sell. In just a moment I will show you exactly where to properly use the word "and" instead of 'but".

If customer tells you that the interest rate is too high.

Kenneth I agree, the interest rate is a little higher than what you had in mind and (instead of but) if you make sure you make the payments on time for at least a year you can refinance the loan and drop the interest rate to a number you will feel good about.

If customer tells you they want more for the vehicle they are trading in.

Roger I agree, you feel you should get more for your trade and keep in mind, where not saying this is what your trade is worth all we are saying is that based on the current market this is the offer we are able to give you. Which is a strong offer. Go ahead and sign here for me.

If customer tells you that the price of your training course is expensive.

Ryan, I agree, this course is expensive and that is why it is packed full of useful information you can implement now. Sign here.

If client tells you the listing you are looking at is more expensive than another listing.

I agree, this home is more expensive and the issue isn't about it being more expensive, because they are both in your budget, this issue is which one do you want to own?

Customer tells you that the insurance policy is expensive.

I agree, this insurance policy is more expensive and that is why it will give you peace of mind knowing you are completely covered if anything happens. Do you want your wife as the beneficiary?

Client tells you the home you are showing is out of their budget.

I agree this house is a little more than you budgeted for and that is why it has everything you are looking for and more. Go ahead and sign here before anyone else puts in an offer.

If customer tells you that they have to talk to their wife or husband.

I agree and you should, and what do you think your wife will say if you did buy here this beautiful car, got a great deal and you had 5 days to drive the car just to make sure it is the right one? Tell you what, you don't even have to answer that. You seem like a man who makes smart decisions. Sign here and I will get it ready for you while we finish up the paperwork.

Customer tells you they have to speak with their spouse or someone else involved in the decision.

I agree, and we both know that it is better to ask for forgiveness than for permission. Sign here. (and just smile)

Customer tells you that product or service is more than they had in mind.

I agree this is more than you had in mind. But I'm sure this isn't the first time you spent more than you expected on something you want, is it?

Customer tells you that the product or service is more than they expected to spend.

I agree this is more than you expected to spend on something you want and I'm sure it won't be the last. Everyone does it. Sign here.

Customer tells you the furniture set is expensive.

I agree this expensive. Be grateful that you can purchase a room setting like this. Not everyone can purchase furniture this nice. I wish I could. How is Friday afternoon for delivery?

Customer tells you that the training for their company is more than they wanted to spend.

I understand that it's more money than you wanted to spend. Do it anyway, because we both know great service isn't cheap and cheap service isn't great.

Customer gives you a low ball number and says he will do the deal if you accept the offer.

I like where your head is at and if I was in your shoes I would have come up with the same numbers, and we both know I can't do those numbers and we both know this is a great deal. Sign here.

<u>Other Than</u>

(This one is simple, to the point, and has been used since the beginning of selling.)

Other than (X) is there anything else holding you back from moving forward with the deal toady?

Once you have a commitment that, whatever the objection is, is the only issue holding them back from making the purchase, handle it. The worst thing for a salesperson to do is not ask what the concern is. Think about it for a moment. How will you know what problem to resolve if you do not know what the problem is? The problem could be something as simple as wanting to take delivery at a later time or wanting the item in a different color. You never know until you ask.

If a customer tells you that he/she doesn't like the color of the car.

Other than the color is there anything else holding you back from moving forward with the purchase today?

If the customer says they do not like the payment.

Other than the payment is there anything else holding you back from moving forward with the purchase today?

<u>I Completely Understand</u>

Here is a variation of simply acknowledging a "complaint objection" with I completely understand.

• I completely understand where you are coming from. Sign here.

• I completely understand where you are coming from. A few of our happiest customers felt the same way before they purchased. Sign here.

- I completely understand where you are coming from. A few of our happiest customers felt the same way before they purchased from us. What day this week would you like delivery?

I Can Appreciate

- I can appreciate you wanting a better deal, if I were you I would do the same thing, and that is why you can appreciate the deals we have are the best deals. That is why everyone does business with us.

- I can appreciate you wanting a lower interest rate, if I were you I would do the same thing and that is why I know you appreciate that based upon your credit at the moment this is the best interest rate available. Let's build your credit together. Sign here.

- I can appreciate you wanting time to think it over. That just means you do not want to make a wrong decision, right? Well let me ask you the three questions that will help you know if this is the right decision for you. Do you like this car/home? Can afford this car/home? And, I am the type of person you would do business with, right? Perfect. It sounds like this is the right decision for you. Sign here.

- I can appreciate you wanting to talk to your spouse that means you value his/her opinion. And I'm sure that if you are like me and my wife that you have already discussed this purchase with them before you came which means they trust your opinion. Go ahead and sign here and show him/her the great deal you got.

- I can appreciate you wanting to take some time and think it over as I'm sure it is to only make sure you are making the right decision. But by not making the decision now and implementing our sales training for your employees could cause you to lose valuable deals and a decrease in company morale due to low sales, but if you do hire me to train your salespeople then you will begin to see vast improvement in their persuasion abilities and first hand watch your team close more deals. This will boost company morale and everyone's income. A win win for everyone, don't you agree? I need your approval here, so we can get your team started right away.

- I can appreciate you wanting to take some time to think it over as I'm sure it is to only make sure you are making the right decision, right? And we both know sooner or later you have to make a decision, right? And I'm sure that a person like you has other things that require your attention don't you? Well, let me ask you. Do you like the software? Do you feel your company can benefit from it? Am I the type of person you would do business with? Good. The sooner we do this the better it will be for you and your company. Sign here and we will get started right away.

On One Level It's X And On Another Level It's

- On one level the interest rate is higher that you expected but on another level you have a strong approval and can drive your new car home today. Sign here and I will get it washed up for you and a full tank of gas.

- On one level the price is a little more than you were looking to spend but on another level this home is everything you are looking for.

- On one level the this retirement plan grows a little slower than you wanted but on another level it give you the long term security you are looking for.

- On one level my sales training is expensive but on another level it is packed full of powerful information. And you want to make a smart investment don't you? Sign here.

- On one leve_ this sales course is expensive but on another leve_ it will teach you a number of powerful techniques to close more deals and earn more money. And, after all, that is what you wanted from a sales course, isn't it? Sign here.

- On one level the appraised value of your truck is not as much as you wanted but on another level it is a strong offer and you do not have to spend a lot of your time trying to sell it on your own. Go ahead and sign here and I will get a check cut for you now.

- On one level you have the option of running around spending countless hours dealing with those other car salespeople and trying to beat our deal and on another level you could save yourself a lot of precious time, feel good about the car and deal you have now. Sign here and I will get the paperwork started for you.

How to overcome objections is one of the most frequently asked questions by salespeople, and one of the most important questions for salespeople. Because, let's face it, most customers have objections and by not equipping yourself with the most persuasive and hypnotic sales techniques available it is costing you, your business, and your family money. Knowing how to overcome objections and learning a few powerful hypnotic sales closes are a definite way of opening that door of success and a larger bank account.

I have said it before and I will say it again, practice, practice, practice. Practice is the pathway to success.

Practice overcoming objections, write the objections down and the sentence structures that will stop them in their tracks so they cannot be used. Practice the closes, role play closes with other salesmen or friends. Remember, when you are not sharpening your skills, someone else is. If you want to be the best, learn the best techniques and then practice them over and over again. Practice until you do not have to think about how to say them. Practice them until they are a natural part of your speech.

Whatever you think you sell forget it. You sell feelings. If you control the feelings you control the sell.

CHAPTER 8

VISUALIZE THE SALE

"You begin by always expecting good things to happen."

Tom Hopkins

Visualize

I want you to think about this question for a moment. Where did the product you sell to your customers, the car you drive to the beach, and the boat you take to the lake, all first begin? Here, let me tell you. They were all first created in someone's imagination. That's right, everything begins in the mind's eye.

The clothes you are wearing, the phone you do everything with, the home you live in, they were all first created in the mind. Imagination is raw power in its simplest form.

Someone had to first visualize the product or service in their mind's miracle factory before it could be manifested. According to the Merriam-Webster dictionary, imagination is *"the act or power of forming a mental image of something not present to the senses or never before wholly perceived in reality."* You see, the imagination is really where reality is created.

With your imagination, you begin to create the world and the wealth around you. You think, therefore, you create. It's that simple. So, if it is that simple, why not visualize and create the entire sales process from greeting to close going smoothly, efficiently, and effortlessly?

If everything is first created in the mind's eye, then why not visualize closing more sales than anyone in your company? Why not visualize your checking account with one, two, or even ten million dollars in it? Why not? Who says you can't? The great thing that you are beginning to learn now is that you can be a part of this incredible process of creating wealth, prosperity, and your financial future. Have you started to see yourself creating the life of your dreams?

Visualize and Make More Money

Visualization is one of the most simple and most powerful techniques used around the world. In fact, it is so simple that most simple-minded individuals will simply ignore it. Most people (the 80%) look for the most complicated solution to a problem, while the successful individuals look for what will be the most efficient, easiest, and most profitable solution. And visualization, when done properly, is that solution. However, before we go into how to properly execute this technique, I want to go over a few things with you.

Why does it always seem that it's just a select few salesmen that make all the money and close their sales with ease while others struggle to even make a paycheck? The answer is simple. It's because the successful sales professionals know they are going to close their deals. The sales process has already taken place in their mind. They have already visualized the outcome of the sale, and they have already visualized their customers being completely satisfied and sending them referrals. It was already over before it even began.

The mind is constantly working to create the reality that it is shown. It is your God-given birthright to discover and use this inner power of thought and emotion. The key to the power that you have hidden inside of you can unlock the doors of financial abundance in your life. Once this knowledge is achieved and applied, the world and its wealth will readily be at your fingertips.

Your Magical Genie

Your mind is your personal servant and it works to make sure your life is consistent with your internal dialogue and the images you create. If you are constantly thinking and visualizing closing the sale, then the mind will manifest you constantly closing the sale.

If you constantly think of all the things that could possibly go wrong and why the prospect will not buy from you, then guess what, you will experience the prospect giving you reasons why they will not buy your product or service. It's that simple. Ask and it shall be given unto you. Be sure to clearly and positively ask for what you want.

The reason for this is that if your mind does not create and manifest what it is shown, and you experience situations that contradict these images that you believe to be true, then you will think that you are crazy, and your mind will not let this happen.

Look at it like this. Your mind, more specifically, your subconscious mind, which is documented to make up 99.994% of your mind, is a genie with a huge ego. Your personal genie is what dictates the results you get in life. Your conscious mind commands and your subconscious obeys. It is strong, powerful, and is always right. Your subconscious mind will say, "I'm not going to let anything happen to contradict what I believe to be true. I am perfect. If you are showing me that you live an opulent and affluent life, then I must create it. If you are showing me that you are lazy and have lack, then I create that too. Your wish is my command."

The mind creates what it is shown and believes to be true in your heart of hearts. Take this for example, have you ever had a job interview or a prospect you were with and you just felt completely confident with and absolutely knew deep down inside that everything was going to go perfectly and with ease, and it did? The company gave you the position on the spot or you got the sale and the customer just loved you and wound up sending you numerous high grossing referrals. Well, this is visualizing in action. What you visualize and feel to be true will be true.

This is extremely important, be careful what you tell your mind to create because your mind will not discern right from wrong or good from bad, and then select what would be the best option for you. It will only create what you tell it to create. You, my friend, are the owner of this powerful reality-creating machine; use it to your benefit. Do not be one of those salesmen who will give every reason in the book why a prospect couldn't buy and then wonder why they can't pay their bills. I challenge you to be the sales professional who finds the reason the customer can and will buy and then close them.

If you want an abundance of sales, clients lined up at your door, and a bank account bursting at the seams, then use the powerful technique of visualization to create it. Oprah Winfrey uses it. Tyler Perry uses it. Even athletes use this technique all the time to improve their skill level. They are taught this valuable secret early on in their career, and the ones who truly grasp the understanding of it and apply the technique become the superstar athletes and this is the reason why they dominate their arena so easily.

How to Visualize

In the article, *Teaching Athletes Visualization and Mental Imagery Skills* written by Dr. David Yukelson of Penn State University, he says, "Many athletes use imagery as a mental training skill to build confidence and a feeling of readiness prior to the competition. It can also be used as a cognitive technique to plan competition strategies, rehearse game plans, affirm what you want to occur, or as a coping skill strategy to stay calm and composed under pressure. Everyone possesses the ability to use imagery, like anything else, it is a skill that must be developed and practiced."

In the same article, Dr. Yukelson explains the crucial element that most people are missing for the power of visualization to work. Dr. Yukelson says, "The key is to program your mind, muscles, and emotions for success, and to make your imagery as vivid, realistic, and detailed as possible. When you vividly imagine yourself getting ready for competition, your central nervous system becomes programmed for success. With authentic practice and specific application it's as if the activity you visualized has already happened!"

According to Nicole Detling, a sports psychologist with the United States Olympic team, "The more an athlete can imagine the entire package, the better it's going to be." This is true for all of us, not just athletes. The more vividly we create the image in the theater of our mind, the more we are programming ourselves for what it is we want! The more we visualize the entire picture, the better it's going to be. We can use this simple technique for the entire sales process and our financial freedom!

There was a case study where two businessmen had a product to sell: luxury mattresses. The first fellow decided to approach as many retailers as he could to get his mattress in their stores. Through a lot of struggle and hard work, he eventually got a few contracts, but the money did not flood into his account very quickly, and he was easily discouraged. Unfortunately for this first businessman, he never reached his goal of making $500,000 because he soon gave up on his tiring venture.

The second fellow did something very different. He spent a few days thinking about how he would sell his mattresses. While the first guy was out pounding the pavement, this second businessman spent his days lounging around in his garden, thinking of innovative ways to sell his mattresses. He ended up creating an interesting marketing system that landed him big accounts with various hotels. Consequently, the money started flooding into his bank account very quickly and furiously. He was happy indeed. He met his goal of making $500,000 profit and in fact, exceeded it!

(Article from UpstartSuccess.com)

All you have to do is take 5 minutes and use your imagination. Use your imagination to visualize what you want in your life, use it vividly with emotions to see the life you want to have as if you already have it. From time to time, I have had some people tell me that they cannot visualize and if you are one of those people who think they cannot visualize, then I do not want you to try to visualize for this exercise.

All I want you to do is simply recall one of your fondest memories. It could be your childhood sweetheart, your first car, your favorite toy, or even your bedroom as a kid. I want you to recall this memory. What did it look like? What do you see? How do you feel when you recall this memory? Now, I want you to realize something, you just used visualization. It's nothing complicated. It is simple.

The powerful technique of visualization is simple and can be very exciting. Truthfully, it is like being a child all over again. You get to imagine anything you want and no one can stop you. The only person that can limit your imagination is you. The only person that can limit your income potential is you. So, you must remember to watch your thoughts, because they will become your world.

Once you begin visualizing and start to see your internal thoughts manifest into external experiences, the more your confidence and finances will grow, and the easier it will be for you to manifest even more. Think about it. I'm sure the first time you drove a car was pretty nerve racking, wasn't it?

First, you nervously get in and adjust the seat and mirrors, hoping they are in the perfect position because you know you will need them shortly. You grab the key and slide it into the ignition, and slowly turn it until you hear the car start up, which stirs up excitement and anxiousness in the pit of your stomach.

Soon, you will be driving down the road heading to your destination with other cars whizzing by you, and there will be turns to take and stops to make along the way. You put it into gear and slowly press the gas, looking in all directions just to make sure there are no other vehicles that can interfere with your journey. And all this is before you even get out of the driveway.

However, the more you drove, the more your confidence grew, and the easier it became for you and before you knew it, you were in autopilot driving without having to consciously think about it.

Visualization is the same way and you can visualize your way to the top. Visualize a close with every person you speak to. Not only a close, but that you make a great commission on the deal and your client or customer is extremely happy with you and your service or product, and continually sends you referrals.

Visualize closing the sale, and then visualize the next prospect coming in through the door or calling and closing them. Then visualize the next and then the next one after that. Visualize your checking account growing larger and larger and visualize it all as if you already have it. Visualize everything you want to be as if it already is. Visualizing in present tense is key, and before you know it, like driving a car, you will be in autopilot, closing every sale and living the life that was once just a dream.

Visualize whatever it is you desire in perfect detail. Get all of your senses involved because the more involved all your senses are, the better. You want your emotions to be fully engaged. The stronger the emotions and the clearer the visualization is, the better. Remember, your mind only knows what you tell it to be true and will act accordingly. Begin by sowing the seeds of greatness, closing every deal, prosperity, and gratitude in your mind now. Accept them fully, NOW!

Picture your perfect life playing out as if you are already living it. Picture yourself heading home after a great day at work doing the job you truly love, after closing deal after sweet deal. See yourself driving your dream car along the winding roads until you reach your driveway and picture yourself slowly pulling up in that beautifully landscaped driveway, where you park in the first bay of your 3-car garage.

See yourself happily walking over and opening the front door of your new home, and then hearing the sound of the door closing behind you. See your perfect companion greeting you with a smile and an embracing hug that just resonates love through and through. Feel the smile on your face as you gaze out of the floor-to-ceiling windows at the back of the house and catch the sun setting. Feel all the joy and love of living in the home you always dreamed of with the one you always dreamed of. Feel successful and fulfilled.

Be detailed when you visualize. The more detail and emotion you put in, the stronger it will become and the more quickly it can manifest. You are the creator of your reality. Visualize it in detail and with great emotion and get ready for the creation to begin.

Reality is relative. The reality you create and live is your perception of reality. The title or label you give a situation is that and only that because it is what you titled or labeled the particular instance. A bad situation is only bad because you labeled it bad and a circumstance is great because you labeled it great.

Your mind is a gift from God and this gift that you have been blessed with is overflowing with the Infinite Power of God, which includes the power to change, the power to influence, the power to prosper, the power to create happiness, and more. They are all there for you to control if you understand how. Anything you desire to have is readily available to you once you understand the formula and make the choice to believe it to be true.

You have to remember that the secret is to get your emotions involved. The mind only knows what you are telling it. It cannot distinguish the difference between past and the future, true or false, imagination from reality. It only knows what you tell it and how you feel about what you are telling it, and it works to create that as your reality. Your life will be what you feel and what you show yourself in the movie of your mind.

CHAPTER 9

THE POWER OF GRATITUDE

"The more you express gratitude for the things you have, the more things you have to express gratitude for."

Zig Ziglar

As the famous motivational guru Zig Ziglar often said, "You must have an attitude of gratitude." Gratitude is one of the most important key principles in *The Formula for Success in Sales*. Withholding gratitude is the equivalent of having a dam in the middle of a powerful river, the water wants to flow freely, but can't due to the blockage.

Remove the blockage and let the river of abundance flow freely in your life.

Have an Attitude of Gratitude

Think about this for a moment. If you are not grateful for what you have, then why should you be given more? If you are not grateful for the customer or client who just gave you their business, which allows you to provide for your family, enables you to live the life you are accustomed to, and put food in your mouth and money into your checking account, then why should you have another one?

Possessing the attitude of gratitude will open the door of abundance of the universe and allow abundance to flow to you, instead of you ceaselessly chasing after it. God has infinite power and unlimited resources. The vast universe has no end from which we can see and functions perfectly without any help. If the creator created the entire universe and all of the galaxies and planets, and everything inside the earth, including you and me, and everything in between, all the way down to the minutest detail such as microorganisms and atoms and energy, don't you agree that it is possible for him to create a healthy financial future for you?

You see, we, with our limited thinking, put limitations on what we can achieve in life. We are the ones who say we cannot earn more money. We are the ones who say no one is buying right now. We are the ones who say there are no jobs out there and the economy is bad. We are the ones who prejudge a prospect as soon as we see or speak to them. I challenge you now to shed yourself of the financial life-sucking limitations, and give thanks for the blessings you already have, and watch an increase come your way. After all, you do want an increase, don't you?

What exactly is gratitude? Gratitude is simply the quality of being thankful and the readiness to show appreciation for, and to return kindness. It sounds simple enough, doesn't it? To return kindness and show thanks for what you have. Unfortunately, for some, this simple principle has been lost and forgotten.

I'm sure you know some of these people. They withhold from any and every one in need and they feel as if the world is out to get them and their money, even if they have no money. Now, don't get me wrong, I'm not saying that because you have money, you are required to give all of your money away. That would be silly. You earned it, enjoy it. What I am saying is be grateful for what you have. Giving can be a number of things and you can give in the form of money, time, advice, service of some sort, or even just a shoulder to lean on.

If you do not possess this powerful life-changing principle success is going to be just out of reach for you. You will continue to thirst for more, never being fulfilled and this thirst will not be quenched until you are happy with what you already have and show appreciation for it.

You will also notice, if you do not have gratitude, happiness will also be missing from your life. If you are unhappy with what you have now, then you will not be happy with what you will obtain in the future. If you are not happy with who you are now, then you will not be happy with who you will become in the future. It is that simple because having all the money and success only changes the outside circumstances, if you are not first grateful for the things you do have, then none of it matters.

Brad Pitt is famous and known for his good looks as well as being a talented actor and producer. According to most of the world's standards, it would appear he has it all, good looks, fortune, fame, a beautiful wife, and a loving family. However, in an interview with Rolling Stone magazine, he had this to say, "I'm telling you, once you've got everything, then you're just left with yourself. I've said it before and I'll say it again: it doesn't help you sleep any better, and you don't wake up any better because of it."

It doesn't matter who you are or what you have; if you are not first happy on the inside and grateful for what you have, then you can gain everything underneath the sun and you will still not be satisfied. If your spirit is empty and unhappy, tangible possessions will not quench that thirst.

Now, I'm not saying Brad Pitt is not grateful or unhappy, I don't know Brad and have not had the luxury to speak with him, but I do know that even with all of the "things" he has accrued, like so many others, he still has that empty feeling inside.

"Be thankful for what you have; you'll end up having more. If you concentrate on what you don't have, you will never, ever have enough."

Oprah Winfrey

Forgiveness

What we are discussing in this chapter may seem a little different from what you will see in most books that teach how to become successful in the field of sales, and that is a good thing. That is what you want. There are tons of books out there that cover techniques, but how many truly discuss the principles? Just because you know all the words to a song doesn't mean you can be a professional singer. This book goes deeper and gives you not only the techniques, but also the principles, because after all, and trust me, these principles are paramount to your obtaining the financial freedom you desire.

Now let's talk about forgiveness. It would seem that the forgiver holds the position of power because the forgiver is the one who can either grant forgiveness or withhold it, right? However, in reality, true power is gained by the act of forgiving in itself. Holding on to thoughts that produce negative emotions such as mistakes you have made, betrayals by someone you trusted, or being done wrong by another salesman or manager, will only cause you not to heal and ultimately rob you of your blessings. Holding onto negativity will poison you emotionally and financially.

Buddha once said, "Holding on to bitterness and unforgiveness is like drinking poison and expecting the other person to die." The one who consumes the poison is the one who will be poisoned – no one else. So why do so many of us get caught up in drinking the poison of unforgiveness? Because forgiveness can be a tough, pride-filled pill to swallow, and we just do not want to force that big pill down our throats.

It can also be a pill that takes off the blinders to reality and grants self-awareness, and some people just do not want that. Some people have found their identity in all the hurt, and whether they know it or not, do not want to let it go. They feel it gives them a reason to act the way they do, or a reason they failed at something in life, or a reason they cannot achieve and excel in life.

The Bible says in 1 Thessalonians 5:18, "Be joyful always, pray continually, and give thanks in all you do for this is God's will for you in Christ Jesus." If we are grateful, it will bring us closer to God, The Infinite Power. The closer we are to the source, the stronger and more powerful we are.

Benefits of Gratitude

The benefits of gratitude have been studied by scientists, doctors, and professionals across the globe. Here is a graph from Happierhuman.com from their article "The 31 Benefits of Gratitude you didn't know about: How Gratitude can change your life" by Amit Amin. The graph shows the benefits of gratitude.

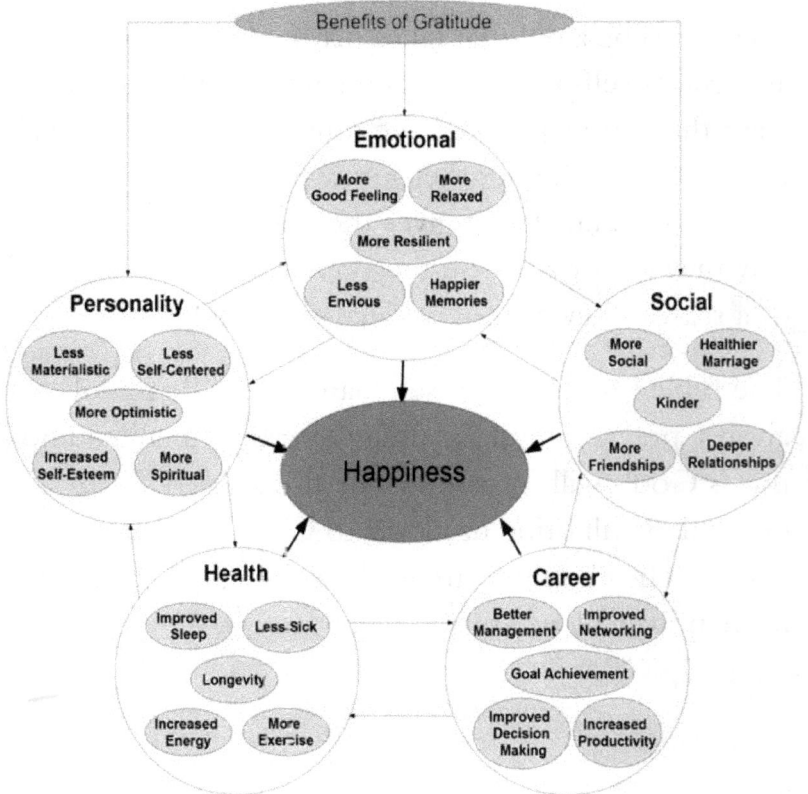

According to Dr. Robert A. Emmons, "Gratitude research is beginning to suggest that feelings of thankfulness have tremendous positive value in helping people cope with daily problems, especially stress."

Those that live in a constant state of gratitude always seem to have, to be happy, and not to mention are a lot easier to be around than those who are always complaining. Dr. Emmons goes on to say, "Grateful people take better care of themselves and engage in more protective health behaviors like regular exercise, a healthy diet, and regular physical examinations."

For a lot of people, good quality sleep is hard to come by, especially for those in the sales profession because they are always ruminating over a deal and wondering if it is going to close on time and without any problems. Research done by Psychology Today has shown that by taking a few minutes every night before bed to jot down a few things you are grateful for, you will not only fall asleep faster, but you will also sleep longer. This is an especially great exercise for those who have trouble sleeping or falling asleep. The better quality sleep you get, the better chance you have at feeling great the next day and closing that deal that requires a little more effort.

Life is what you focus on. Here, let me show you. Imagine you took your camera and went throughout your business, taking pictures all day long. If you only focused on the salesmen that were not closing deals and prospects who answered with the dreaded, "just looking" response, then you and everyone else you showed the pictures to would picture the business you are in as tough and extremely difficult to make any money. On the other hand, if instead, you only focused on the salesmen who were closing deals, customers happily engaging in conversation with other sales professionals, and referrals walking through the doors, then you and everyone you showed the pictures to will see a business that is booming with growth and opportunity and an abundance of money to be made. Your profession and opportunities will be determined by what you focus your camera lens of life on. Focus on the right picture and you will get the right outcome.

Focus on being grateful for what you have instead of what you do not have. Those who are grateful will be given more. If you focus on lack, then you will bring more lack into your life, whether it is lack of money, time, friends, good health, etc. Oprah Winfrey stated it very clearly, "The single greatest thing you can do to change your life today would be to start being grateful for what you have right now. And the more grateful you are, the more you get." Oprah knows something about selling and gratitude, she owns her own network and Forbes has estimated her net worth to be over two billion dollars.

The Law of Attraction states that you bring to your life what you think about most. What you believe you deserve, you will receive. The thoughts we send out have a certain vibrational frequency and will return with what it was sent out to retrieve. If you are thinking lack, you will bring lack. So, why not think abundance? What will it hurt? Would it be so bad to have an abundance of all the good things life has to offer?

It is healthy for you to want more and to do more in life. It is okay to want a bigger house, to want to earn more money, or have a vacation home on every continent, well except Antarctica unless you like the igloo life. That is what keeps people motivated and wanting more, but remember, if you are not grateful for where you are, who you are, and for what you have right now, then you will not be happy with more.

I want you to understand something; I'm not talking about being grateful just to receive more, that is greed and being greedy will not only cause the Law of

Reciprocation to stop, but it can and will also cause you to lose friends and the respect from your peers.

Rhonda Byrne puts it this way, "Be grateful for what you have now. As you begin to think about all the things in your life you are grateful for, you will be amazed at the never-ending thoughts that come back to you of more things to be grateful for. You have to make a start, and then the law of attraction will receive those grateful thoughts and give you more just like them." I am now going to give you a few exercises to implement in your life.

Get Rid of Negativity

Get rid of the negativity in your life, it will only rob you of sales. The news and media are full of the negativity all around the world. They force feed you all the economic woes, crimes, terroristic news, and anything negative that is available from every corner of the globe. If this is all you see, then your view of life will be one of despair and hopelessness and it without a doubt will negatively impact your sales, unless of course, you are selling doomsday supplies.

Limit the amount of time you spend with negative friends or salesmen or completely get rid of them altogether. They are like a virus and will eventually attack the functioning of your brain and cause you to view the world the same as they do, with a negative filter. They are only able to see the negativity life has to offer, which in turn, only attracts more negative experiences, situations, and people. Focusing on the negative is a sure way for you to make sure you do not make any money.

Close your eyes, or your camera lens on life, and then open them. How do you see the world? This is your world; it is exactly how you want to see it, exactly what you think it is. If you believe there are not enough opportunities and that everyone you work with will snake you and you continue to focus on bad situations either from your workplace or from stories you have heard to reinforce that belief, then I guarantee you that you will create that world to live in.

If you believe there is opportunity and growth, and that customers love to do business with you and focus on positive situations to reinforce that belief, you will also create that world. How? From your very own personal genie. Remember we discussed your personal genie in the previous chapter.

Don't get me wrong, I'm not trying to suggest living in a fantasy world and that you will never face negative life experiences. No one is immune to the difficulties of life. What I am saying is that if you focus on the good and are grateful for what you have and where you are in life, then you will begin to notice more to be grateful about, thus creating more positive experiences and situations to occur in your life.

Tough situations are only temporary. It can't rain forever, the sun has to come out and shine at some point. I want you to take a moment and think about the worst time in your life. It could have been a breakup, a death of someone close to you, losing your job, or being homeless. It was a bad time in your life, wasn't it? And yet, still, here you are because life goes on and it will continue to go on. You can look at all the things in life you have to be grateful for and enjoy each passing day, or you can simply be negative and let life pass you by. It is your choice.

Life will go on whether you are healthy or sick, wealthy or broke, grateful or not. In life, there are setbacks, losses, deaths, and disappointments. Life is not perfect, but without experiencing the negative, we can't truly appreciate the positive in life. If you have always been wealthy your entire life and never once experienced lack, you would not truly appreciate the level of wealth you have.

Change Your Focus

If you change your thoughts, then you can change your world. Once you begin to notice things you are grateful for, instead of what you don't like or are unhappy with at the present moment, you will begin to see more things you are grateful for. Things you may have been taking for granted and were not even aware of and this is when a transformation will take place in your life. Your mind will create new neurological receptors that will allow you to become more aware and appreciate the large and small things in life on a more consistent basis.

Changing your thoughts is like walking through a tall wheat field. The first pass through will be faint and not very visible, but the more passes you make through the same trail, the easier it will be seen and the less you have to search for it. Soon, it will be so apparent that you will see it automatically without having to search for it.

This new awareness has the ability to single-handedly change your life for the better. It has the potential to allow for the steady flow of abundance from the universe to you. Like everything else in life, this skill isn't necessarily given at birth, it is one that needs to be practiced. It has to be conditioned; like learning closing techniques in sales or selecting the proper foods to eat for a balanced diet, it should be practiced.

What I have found in my research is that those who are grateful for what they have enjoy life on a much deeper and more connected level. They are more connected with the Creator, with others, and with themselves. Their lives are more fulfilled and joyful. If you, like them, look for the small things in life to be grateful about, the big things will be even bigger.

Now, I'm not going to go in depth on ways for you to notice what you have to be grateful for, because we are adults, and since you are reading this book, you know what you have to be grateful for. However, I am going to give a few examples that you can highly benefit from doing. Many of my clients have used these simple exercises and reported great results.

Here are three simple, but powerful exercises to help you become aware of the things to be grateful for. These exercises will allow you to remove the dam that is blocking up your river of abundance.

Ask Quality Questions

(Remember, disempowering questions get disempowering answers. Quality questions get quality answers.)

What am I grateful for in my relationship?

What am I grateful for concerning my health?

What am I grateful for in my job?

What am I grateful for in my career field?

What am I grateful for in my home?

What am I grateful for in my abilities?

What am I grateful for in my means of transportation?

What am I grateful for in my family?

What am I grateful for in my friends?

What am I grateful for in my spirituality?

Everyone has something to be grateful for. Write down these questions and their answers on a piece of paper. If at first you can only think of one answer, write it down. If you can think of ten, even better, write them down.

Keep a Gratitude Journal

The sole purpose of this journal will be for writing about the things you are grateful for on a daily basis. It could be the phone call from a friend or client you haven't heard from in a while, or the time with family. It could be the job promotion, it doesn't matter. There are no right or wrong answers to write down, as long as you are grateful for them. Some days, you will have more things to be grateful for than others, but try to write a minimum of five things every day.

Here are a few of the benefits of keeping a gratitude journal as reported from Happierhuman.co

Benefits at a Glance

Results1	Study	Date
Keeping a gratitude journal caused participants to report **16% fewer physical symptoms, 19% more time spent exercising, 10% less physical pain, 8% more sleep, and 25% increased sleep quality**	Counting Blessings Versus Burdens	2003
The emotions of appreciation and gratitude shown to **induce the relaxation response.**	The Grateful Heart	2004
A gratitude visit **reduced depressive symptoms by 35% for several weeks**, a gratitude journal **lowered depressive symptoms by 30%+** for as long as the practice was continued.	Positive Psychology Progress	2005
Patients with hypertension were instructed to count their blessings once a week. There was a **significant decrease in their systolic blood pressure**	Gratitude Effects on Perspectives and Blood Pressure	2007
Gratitude correlated with **improved sleep quality** $(r = .29)$, **less time required to fall asleep** $(r = .20)$, and **increased sleep duration** $(r = .14)$.	Gratitude Influences Sleep Through the Mechanism of Pre-Sleep Cognitions	2009
Levels of gratitude significantly correlated with **vitality and energy.**	Multiple Studies	Many

"A five-minute-a-day gratitude journal can increase your long-term well-being by more than ten percent. That's the same impact as doubling your income!" Amit Amin of happierhuman.co

<u>Take the 7-Day Challenge</u>

Begin to unlock the floodgates of gratitude with this challenge. This 7-day challenge is one of the most powerful exercises you can involve yourself in.

Make a commitment to yourself that you will not complain, criticize, or involve yourself in any kind negative talk for seven days, and that for seven days, you will commit to writing seven things you are grateful for in your gratitude journal and smile for one minute seven times a day. If you forget to write in your journal or realize that you have complained, criticized, or involved yourself in negative talks, then you must start over. The same goes for smiling.

If gratitude is consistent and continuous, then that which you are to be grateful for will be consistent and continuous. If you go to work consistently at the same time, every day and end at the same time every day, then your paycheck will be continuous. Stop going to work and you will stop getting paid. The only difference is one will pay you back what you believe you are worth, while the other will only pay you what someone feels your position is worth.

CHAPTER 10

THE 7 STEPS TO SUCCESS IN SALES PROCESS

The 7 Steps To Sales In Process

By now, you should be feeling very confident with the newly gained knowledge you possess and in your ability to dominate the sales industry and have complete and total success in sales. You have just learned a tremendous amount of valuable information that only the top 10% of sales professionals know and use to create their results.

By now you have learned how to instantly build rapport with everyone you meet. You have learned the covert techniques of fact finding and how to create powerful elevator pitches for those times when time is of the essence. You have also learned hypnotic closing techniques that are proven to work and let's not forget the power of gratitude, visualization, and motivation. These are absolutely powerful principles to be used if you want to achieve amazing financial gains in your life.

Now time recap the 7 Steps To Success In Sales Process in the same order that top salesmen around the world use to get their unbelievable results.

1. Motivation. Motivation is your motives in action. Motives are the reasons you want to take action, your *why*. In order to keep motivated and achieve success your *why* has to be greater than your *how*. If your how is not greater than your why then you will easily be persuaded to procrastinate. Procrastinate long enough and whatever it is you wanted to achieve or accomplish will soon only be a dream you once had. It will only be a thought, a constant reminder of why your life is not where you want it to be. Do not be one of those people who look back on their lives and say, "I wish I would have done XYZ." Create strong enough motives to fuel your drive to accomplish your dreams and you will live the life you desire. You deserve it.

2. Attitude. Attitude is everything. Your attitude will determine if you succeed or fail in sales. In fact it will not only determine if you succeed or fail in sales, but in every other aspect of your life as well. Studies show and individual's success is comprised of 88% attitude and only 12% education. It doesn't matter where you came from, if you have a college degree, and it doesn't matter what race, gender, or religion you are. What matters is your attitude. Your attitude can make you a millionaire or it can make you broke

3. Visualization. Before the sale even begins, technically you should do this before the work day even begins. Take five minutes and visualize how you want your day to be. Visualize the perfect ride in to work (that is if you drive to work), visualize attracting the perfect client or customer who purchases from you easily and effortlessly and sends you an uncountable amount of referrals. Visualize only attracting those people, situations, and events that will be to your benefit. Visualize the perfect day for you.

Remember everything first begins as a thought. Albert Einstein said, "Your imagination is a preview of life's coming attractions." So, why not imagine having and being the best? Five minutes a day could change your life forever.

4. Instantly Build Rapport. Instantly build rapport with every person you come into contact with. Rapport is essential to you selling a product or service and/or to you being accepted into a group. Remember, people like those who are like themselves and rapport is what determines if the other person will be open to what you have to say or turn a deaf ear to you.

The process of matching and mirroring is the strongest covert technique to instantly build rapport. Make a game out of it. The areas to match and mirror are physiology, breathing, tone of voice, metaphors, speech patterns, etc. Learn this and you will instantly gain access to the customer's circle of trust. But remember, do not match and mirror them overtly, do it covertly.

5. Fact Finding. Fact finding is exciting and intriguing. When fact finding is done properly it will enable you to close almost every deal easily and effortlessly due to the amount of emotional buying factors the customer has given you. If you ask the right questions in the right way at the right time you will get the right outcome. Right questions equal right outcome. Wrong question equals wrong outcome. Your choice. By asking the right questions the right way you absolutely become aware of the emotional buying motives of the customer. After all, customers buy with emotions and justify with logic.

If you know the reasons they want a product or service and present it to them the same way they explain it to you, they will feel obligated to give you their business. Why? Because they are dealing with you for a reason, they want your product, and you are giving them exactly what they want. Find their pain and alleviate it. Find out what the customer's desires (hot buttons) for your product or service is and give it to them. It does not get any simpler than that.

6. Closing the Sale. The close is the most important part of the entire sales process, because without this crucial step, nothing happens. The customer does not get to enjoy your product or service and you make absolutely no money. The close is made exceptionally easy if the other steps are performed correctly, but even if they weren't you can still close like a professional with the hypnotic language patterns you learned in Chapter 4. The close is where all the excitement for you and the customer happens The customer is able to purchase the product or service that best suits their wants, needs, and desires and you are able to feel proud about providing your customer with exceptional service and not to mention, collect a handsome commission check. A win win for all parties involved.

7. Gratitude. Gratitude is a principle that all successful athletes, business owners, and sales professionals around the world know and practice. If you are not grateful for what you have, then why should you be given more? Gratitude is the key that will open up the flood gates of abundance into your life. Begin to notice the big and small things in your life to be grateful for. We will attract to us what we focus our attention on. Those that focus their attention on lack will have lack. Those who focus their attention on the things they are grateful for will be given more of those things to be grateful for.

The principle of gratitude has been around since the beginning of time, but only knowing about the principle and not applying it is like knowing that by eating you will not be hungry but questioning why you are always hungry and you never eat. Apply the principle and be prepared to see results.

.

CLOSING

The Formula For Success In Sales was written for you. Everything in life happens for a reason and as you sit there reading this book, looking at the words on this page, you are realizing the reason you are in sales and you are also realizing the persuasive power you now have to close more deals and earn more money and if feels good, doesn't it?

You have learned, from this book and your previous knowledge and experiences, powerful financial changing information that has empowered you to create the financial wealth that most others only dream of. Remember, knowledge isn't power, applied knowledge is power. Empowerment is the key to success and you now have that key.

Every day you get up and your feet hit the floor you should take a deep breath in, smile, and hold your head high because you are a part of the best and most lucrative industry known to man. You belong to an industry that allows you to create the income and wealth you are worth and not what someone says you are worth. Sales. The sales industry is where amateurs are separated from the professionals. And often times what separates the amateurs from the professionals isn't anything huge and grand. The professional salesperson who is making six figures didn't start out the greatest. What they did do though is they learned some of the greatest techniques in sales. The learned techniques pertaining to - attitude, motivation, strategic fact finding, closes, and overcoming objectives. You don't have to know all of the techniques, but you do have to know the ones you feel comfortable with and like. And you don't have to be great at all of them, but you do have to be great at the ones you use.

The formula for success in sales is inside this book. Do not read it once and put it down. If you want to be successful in sales then you want to always keep this book with you and reference back to it often. Read it over and over and complete the exercises inside. If you want to become a professional then you have to act like it. What do professional athletes do? They learn the best techniques and then practice them over and over and over again. That is why they are professionals. That is how they become the greatest. They put in the work and they reap the benefits and rewards. You will do the same if you practice what is inside this book.

On the next page is a little bonus for you. These are **The Top 11 Things The World's Top Salespeople Do To Achieve Success**. If you do these things then you are guaranteed success!

11 Things The World's Top SalesPeople Do To Achieve Success

1.   Develop the mindset of success

2.   Believe in their product and themselves

3.   Follow a proven formula for success

4.   Never stop learning

5.   Grateful for the customers/clients

6.   Have a Million Dollar Sales Script Book

7.   Continue to hone their skills / Practice

8.   Follow up

9.   Perfect their pitch

10.   Stay motivated

11.   Visualize and meditate

I wish you the best in your sales career and would love to hear your success stories. If you have learned anything from this book that may add value to your sales career go to Amazon.com look up this book and leave a comment about the book. It would be greatly appreciated.

Feel free to contact me on my webpage, theformulacoach.com or theformulacoachingsystems.com or my direct email, getformulacoached@gmail.com

Also, you might want to consider reading *The Formula For Happiness And Success In Life*

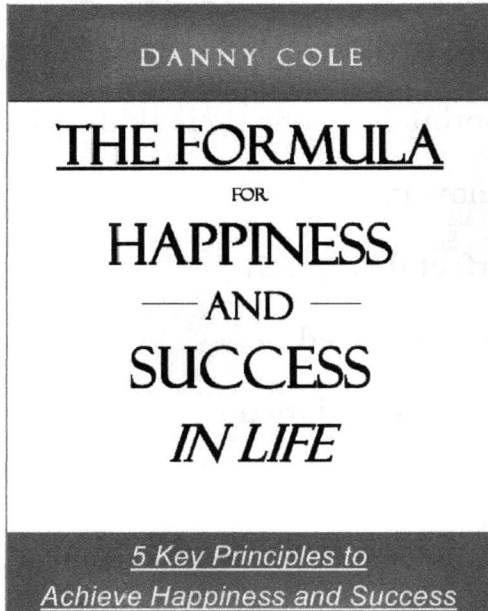

Wishing you happiness and success!